NEW EDITION

Hotter than Hell

Hot & Spicy Dishes from Around the World

by Jane Butel

photography by Christopher Marchetti

NORTHLAND PUBLISHING

To all those who were always at hand to assist with creating, tasting, and developing the recipes, and to Amy, my daughter, who was very helpful and supportive. And, thanks to my Father who inspired it all—he's the one who taught me to like it hot! A special thanks to Lori Greene and Anne Gumina, among others, who were always ready to help put this book in its final form. And, for this second revision and expansion—to my dear agent Sidney Kramer, who has played a vital role in getting this new edition negotiated with a new Publisher, Northland Publishing Inc. Thanks to my fellow employees—Lesley Spring, Tamara Bolek, and Donna Allen, who gladly helped with their own personal ideas, palates, and opinions.

Jane Butel's Hotter Than Hell © 1987 by Jane Butel
Originally published by HPBooks, a division of Penguin Putnam Inc.
Revised Edition © 1994 by Jane Butel

New Edition
Text © 2005 by Jane Butel
Photographs © 2005 by Northland Publishing

www.northlandbooks.com

Composed in the United States of America
Printed in China

Edited by Tammy Gales-Biber
Designed by Dave Jenney
Production supervised by Donna Boyd
Photography by Christopher Marchetti

FIRST IMPRESSION 2005
ISBN 0-87358-883-5

09   08   07   06   05   5   4   3   2   1

Library of Congress Cataloging-in-Publication Data

Butel, Jane.
Hotter than hell : hot and spicy dishes from around the world / Jane Butel.—
New ed.
p. cm.
Includes index.
1. Cookery, International. 2. Spices. 3. Condiments. I. Title.

TX725.A1.B865 2005
641.59—dc22
2004061662

Notice: The information contained in this book is true and complete to the best of our knowledge. All recommendations are made without any guarantees on the part of the Author or Northland Publishing, Inc. The Author and the Publisher disclaim all liability in connection with the use of this information.

CONTENTS

Introduction

Into the Inferno

THE ZINGLY, TINGLY, SINGULARLY EXCITING FLAVORS of piquant spices thrill the palate like nothing else. Ginger, horseradish, mustard, pepper—if you like your food hotter than hell, you know how these spices can liven up dishes of every kind. And for really punishing, pervasive heat, nothing surpasses chiles.

In putting this recipe collection together, I've used these ingredients liberally. You'll find fired-up favorites of all kinds, from appetizers to soups to salads to main dishes. And since all but the most fire-mouthed occasionally crave relief from the heat, I've also included some mild-mannered selections: soothing beverages, side dishes, and desserts.

If your passion for heat is a recent one, you may want to begin by reviewing the basic information on ingredients given in the next few pages. But if you're a long-time aficionado of all things fiery, dig right in and start cooking!

A Guide To Ingredients

Hot, Hot, Hot!

SPICES, ESPECIALLY CHILES, are very good for you! But each of us has a certain preference limit when it comes to spicy foods. However, spiciness—especially from chiles—is addictive: the more you eat, the more you crave. So with such a healthy addiction, it is interesting to know that eating liberal amounts of chiles will also offset the desire for fats, oils, and even salt, all of which can be not as good for you. So spice up your menu with the following hot ingredients.

CHILES

More than 7,000 varieties of chiles grow throughout the world, differing greatly in size and ranging in flavor from pleasantly spicy to downright satanic. Even the spelling of the word varies. I prefer the Spanish spelling, *chile* with a final *-e,* but you'll also see *chili* (to me, that's strictly the name of the dish, as in chili con carne), *chillie,* and even *chilly* or *chilley.*

Another point of confusion concerns the frequent use of the word "pepper" to describe chiles—"hot pepper," "chile pepper," and so forth. Chiles are, in fact, completely unrelated to true pepper *(Piper nigrum);* they belong to the genus Capsicum, which in turn falls into the larger family encompassing potatoes, tomatoes, and eggplant. There's a simple explanation for the "pepper" designation, though. When Spanish explorers first sampled chiles in the Caribbean islands, they likened the amazingly pungent flavor to the black pepper they already knew and named the spicy chile pods accordingly.

Chiles, like bell peppers, turn from green to red (or sometimes yellow or purple) as they ripen; flavor changes, too, from tart and sharp to sweeter and more mellow. In recent years, fresh green chiles have become increasingly available throughout the United States, but ripe, red ones are still sold only regionally and only in autumn. You're far more likely to encounter red chiles in dried form—whole pods, crushed, or ground.

CHOOSING AND HANDLING CHILES

When you're buying fresh chiles, remember this: no two chiles have the same heat level, even if they were plucked from the same plant. Chile bushes cross-pollinate freely, and that can result in variation—up to 35 different piquancies in the fruits on a single stalk. The most reliable key to a chile's nature is its size and shape. Small, narrow-shouldered, deep-colored chiles with pointed tips tend to be the hottest, and larger chiles that are broad across the shoulders are typically milder in flavor.

In buying dried chiles, there's one important rule: go for the real thing! When purchasing crushed and ground chiles, look for lightproof, airtight packaging and, when opened, a fresh, sinus-clearing aroma. And avoid commercial chili powder! Often hot and rank-tasting, it usually contains a mere 40% crushed chiles, with salt, garlic, cumin, oregano, and even corn flour making up the remaining 60%.

Because chiles contain volatile oils that can really burn your skin, you should never tackle them bare-handed. It's especially important to take precautions when you're handling fresh chiles, but the rules apply to dried chiles as well: wear rubber gloves when you prepare chiles, and wash both the gloves and your hands thoroughly with soap and water after you're done. And never, ever rub your eyes, nose, or mouth while you work; the tissue in these areas is extremely sensitive to chile oils.

TYPES OF CHILES

Throughout this book, I've called for only the few types of chiles described below. Some are available in supermarkets, though you'll probably find the best selection in specialty produce stores and Mexican markets. If you can't find the ingredients you need, order them by mail (see sources on page 156) or use the substitutes suggested.

New Mexico Chile

These hybrid chiles are fairly hot and large—about 1 to 2 inches wide at the shoulders, and 5 to 7 inches long. For the best flavor, parch and peel the fresh chiles before use (see Parching Fresh Chiles on page 6). If fresh New Mexico hot green chiles are unavailable, you can generally use canned whole or diced green chiles. (In a few recipes, I've suggested substituting pickled jalapeños to keep the heat level up.)

Dried New Mexico chiles are pulverized, seeds and all, to make the ground pure New Mexico hot red chile called for frequently in my recipes. If you can't find it, substitute commercial crushed hot red pepper. Or make your own ground chile from whole dried pods. Toast the pods in a 325°F oven just until they begin to darken, and then rinse, dry, and stem them. Process the pods, 4 to 6 at a time, in a blender or food processor until finely ground. It's best to prepare only as much ground chile as you need for immediate use. If you do have some leftover, freeze it or store in an airtight, opaque container.

Red Jalapeño Chiles

Jalapeño Chile

These fiery, small to medium-size monsters are beloved by those who like eye-watering heat. When fresh, they're firm, round, dark green or red in color, and about 2 ½ inches long and 1 inch in diameter. If you can't find fresh jalapeños, use the pickled type; they're widely available in most supermarkets.

Serrano Chile

These deep green chiles are tiny (just 1 to 1 ½ inches long), skinny, and hot enough to make you cry! Serrano chiles aren't always easy to find fresh, but you can always use jalapeños in their place.

Serrano Chiles

California (Anaheim) Chile

What was formerly thought of as the California or Anaheim chile has now, once again, been credited to its early beginnings in New Mexico. (The New Mexico chile growers worked to get the credit changed.) And although chiles grown in milder climates—such as California—do take on tamer characteristics, they are essentially New Mexico chiles.

Mild chiles are obtained by either growing a mild variety or by growing chiles in mild weather conditions at a low altitude. Any mild, pure ground chile, whether grown in New Mexico or California, can be substituted for paprika, as it is only slightly hotter and generally redder in color. The fresh chiles should be parched and peeled for use (see page 6) and can be replaced by canned green chiles in cooking. Ground pure California mild red chile is simply powdered dried California chile pods; the seeds are often removed before grinding to assure a milder flavor. Very, very fresh paprika is an acceptable stand-in for ground mild chile used as a garnish. In cooking, though, it's not as hot as the real thing. For best results, try grinding whole dried mild chiles as directed above for New Mexico chiles.

⚜ Poblano (Ancho, Pasilla) Chile

Fresh poblanos look much like bell peppers, but their flavor is much spicier. They're blackish green when fresh, and nearly black when dried. Because they may be difficult to find, I've suggested an alternative in each recipe calling for poblanos—green bell peppers or Italian frying peppers in place of the fresh chiles, or dried whole New Mexico red chiles in place of dried ones.

⚜ Caribe Chile

Grown in northern New Mexico, the caribe is a little larger than the pequín (see below). It's a hot chile with a characteristically sweet, spicy flavor. I call only for crushed dried caribe chile, available by mail order and in some specialty stores. You may substitute commercial crushed hot red pepper for caribe, but the flavor will be milder and less rich.

⚜ Pequín Chile

Extra tiny (just ½ to 1 inch long) and devastatingly hot, these chiles grow wild along the Mexican border. They're potent enough to intimidate all but those with fireproof palates—chiles any more fiery than the pequín are too hot to have any recognizable chile flavor! I have called for them in their crushed dried form, pequín quebrado. Look for pequín quebrado in specialty stores or buy it by mail order. Or, as an easy substitution, use cayenne pepper.

Pequín Chiles

⚜ Other Chiles

In addition to the seven types just discussed, a few other chiles are mentioned in this book. Fresh Oriental hot green chiles, available in Asian markets, are small, thin, and very hot; you may see them sold as Thai Szechwan or Hunan chiles (among other names). Jalapeño or serrano chiles are a good substitute.

Tiny Chinese dried hot red chiles, only about 1 to 1 ½ inches long, are thin and hot. They're quite widely available, both in Asian markets and well-stocked supermarkets. If you can't find them, you can generally substitute an equivalent amount of pure crushed dried hot red chile.

Oriental Chiles

Aromatic, reddish brown dried Szechwan peppers are tiny—about the size of peppercorns—and encased in flowerlike husks. Toasting brings out their fragrance and flavor (see Hot Salt on page 123). You can buy them in Asian markets.

Pickled Tuscan peppers (pepperoncini) are sold in almost every supermarket. They're small yellow-green chiles that are very mild in flavor.

By Italian crushed hot red pepper, I mean the crushed red pepper marketed by major spice companies all over the United States. This product is made from any one of a number of hot chiles, so the heat level may not be consistent from bottle to bottle. Store it in lightproof containers to maintain freshness longer.

PARCHING FRESH CHILES

The true flavor of a chile resides in the flesh of the pod. The ribs and seeds are the source of most of the chile's heat; you can remove them if a milder flavor is desired. The tough skins of large chiles like New Mexico, California, and poblanos should also usually be removed before use, but I don't feel that this is generally necessary with smaller chiles such as jalapeños and serranos. These have thinner skins, and are usually so finely sliced or minced that the skins aren't noticeable in any case.

To parch chiles, begin by dampening a cloth towel and refrigerating it for 30 minutes (or just wrap crushed ice in the towel to chill it). Rinse and drain the chiles, and then pierce each one once near the stem with a sharp knife. If the chile is quite large, pierce it a second time near the tip. Spread the chiles on a baking sheet covered with foil. Broil, turning often, until the skins brown and blister.

As soon as the chiles are evenly browned, remove them from the baking sheet and wrap them in the cold, damp towel. Let them steam for about 10 minutes. If you're using the chiles right away, peel off the skin in long strips. Otherwise, seal the unpeeled chiles in plastic bags and freeze them. The skin will come off easily when the chiles are thawed.

Pull the stem off each peeled chile. To remove the seeds, hold the chile point up, and then squeeze the pod from the point downward. The seeds will easily squirt out.

GINGER

Long an important part of Asian cuisine, this spicy-hot root was also prized by the ancient Romans, who used it lavishly and set its value at 15 times that of pepper. Today, fresh ginger is sold all over the United States, but if it's not consistently available in your local grocery store, you may want to preserve some to guarantee a supply. Just place the root in a jar, add enough dry sherry to cover, and refrigerate. The wine keeps the root from spoiling. (You can use the ginger-flavored sherry in cooking, too.)

Crystallized ginger is also generally available. You can eat it straight, as a sweet-hot confection, or chop it for use in desserts like Butterscotch Peach Crisp on page 151. In a pinch, you may substitute ground ginger for the fresh or crystallized root—the taste won't be as fresh or hot, but it will still have a pleasant zip. As a rule of thumb, use about half as much ground ginger as fresh or crystallized. (Employ this rule only when fairly small amounts are involved. If a recipe calls for ½ cup crystallized ginger, don't shovel in ¼ cup ground; wait until you have the real thing on hand.)

HORSERADISH

There's some dispute over the origin of horseradish. Some say this pungent root first grew in Europe in the area that is now Germany, while others claim it originated in Asia. But no one argues over its value in cooking—it's a marvelous condiment, a zippy addition to sauces, and a delightful garnish for seafood and meat.

My father, a genuine horseradish nut, always bought the fresh root and grated it himself, complaining that purchased brands were often extended with turnips and tasted bland and dull. If you cannot find fresh horseradish (or if you're disinclined to grate it yourself), buy the freshest, purest local brand available. Though commercial preparations are almost always blended with vinegar and salt, with care, you should be able to find a pungent, well-flavored one.

MUSTARD

Mustard has been known since Biblical times for both its peppery-hot greens and its tingly seeds. Originally, the seeds may have been eaten whole—a few seeds with each bite of meat—but today, we typically enjoy them ground and blended with vinegar and other seasonings in prepared mustard.

A great number of commercial mustards are available, varying from sweet to bitingly hot, and from smooth to crunchy. Flavors differ greatly thanks to a wide range of added ingredients, including herbs, honey, horseradish, and various vinegars. If you really like your mustard hot, you may want to make your own—just mix dry mustard to a smooth paste with beer, wine, diluted vinegar, or water. Or doctor up prepared mustard to taste with dry mustard and even whole mustard seeds.

In this book, I have usually called for Dijon-style mustard, which has a sharper flavor than the yellow "ballpark" type. But feel free to substitute another favorite mustard if you like—prepared mustards are really interchangeable in cooking.

PEPPER

When Christopher Columbus discovered the New World, he was searching not for a new land, but for a new and shorter route to the source of black pepper. In Columbus's day—and for many centuries before then—pepper was as negotiable a currency as gold and silver, even preferred over those precious metals in some nations. Today, of course, pepper is no longer expensive, nor is it legal tender! Nonetheless, it's an indispensable seasoning in every kitchen, still prized for the liveliness it lends to all manner of foods.

There are over 2,000 varieties of pepper world-wide. The type most familiar to many of us is *Piper nigrum,* the source of black, white, and green pepper-corns, grown in the hot regions of the world near the equator. To make black pepper, the berries, or corns, are plucked from the vines just before they start to redden, and then they are sun-dried. For white pep-per, the berries are prepared a different way: the black skin is loosened by soaking, and then it is rubbed off, leaving only the hot white center. Green peppercorns are berries picked while still soft and green. They're generally sold pickled or dried in small jars or cans.

For the best, freshest pepper flavor, buy whole black or white peppercorns and grind them yourself. The flat-tasting dust of commercial brands simply can't compare with the sweet hot spiciness of freshly cracked or ground pepper!

OTHER INGREDIENTS

Onions and garlic are integral to good cooking—especially to good HOT cooking. I prefer the hard, round, hot-flavored yellow onions usually called Spanish onions. The flatter, sweeter, softer-textured Bermuda type isn't really emphatic enough. The garlic of choice is the Mexican variety widely sold in supermarkets. Its fairly large cloves are white outside, purplish inside, and have a good hot, pungent taste. Don't use giant-size elephant garlic—it's too mild.

A few recipes call for Mexican oregano. This herb tastes sweeter, milder, and muskier than the Greek or Italian oregano commonly sold by major spice com-panies. Though Mexican oregano isn't yet widely available, you can buy it by mail and at some spice shops, green groceries, and gourmet stores. Especially in Tex-Mex and Mexican dishes, it's best not to sub-stitute regular oregano for the Mexican type—the flavor is too harsh.

Mexican vanilla, stronger by about 1½ times and more flavorful than our domestic brands of vanilla extract, is unsurpassed for use in beverages and desserts. Mexican vanilla is available in the U.S. on a limited basis. Buy only brands that meet Food and Drug Administration guidelines. Use it if you can get it!

ABOUT THE RECIPES

Cooking with hot seasonings is obviously a matter of taste—one man's pain is another man's pleasure. In preparing the recipes in this book, it's a good idea to start with the lowest suggested amount of chiles, horseradish, and so forth, and then slowly work your way up. If you have a number of palates to please, I suggest keeping the heat level relatively low in the dish itself and providing a dish of crushed chiles or other hot seasoning at the table. The real fire-eaters can keep adding until they're satisfied!

The chiles I've used in this book range from mild to searing. The American Spice Trade Association uses Heat Units to rate chiles. On this scale, ground pure mild chiles comes in at 5,000 units, ground pure hot chile at 8,000, caribe at 12,000, and pequín—the hottest of them all—at 40,000! There are much hotter chiles that are generally not as widely available, such as the habanero, which is credited with being the hottest of all chiles at up to 200,000 heat units. In my opinion, they are just too hot to be eaten, unless they are greatly tamed by using just a bit or by adding a lot of acid, such as lime juice. You may find this informa-tion helpful when you are deciding how to adjust each recipe.

A final word. If your mouth is singed from "too much, too hot," ease the pain with dairy fats such as sour cream, butter, cheese, or milk. Sweets are effec-tive, too—there's a good reason why ice cream is the traditional finale to a meal that's hotter than hell!

Appetizers

Light the Fire

WHAT BETTER WAY TO PERK UP WEARY APPETITES than with a spicy, innovative array of appetizers? From Zappo Avocado Appetizers to Crunchy Hot Crab Bites to Instant Bloody Marias, these recipes provide an exciting range of flavors—and most can be prepared with little effort. But even those that require a little more of your time, such as Fluffy Greek Cheese-Chile Pastries, taste so delicious that you just might find yourself making them again and again.

You can adjust the spiciness of all these recipes, making them feistier for chile lovers or milder for tender-mouthed guests. Add or subtract the amount of ground chile and hot-pepper sauce in Cold & Hot Cucumber Canapés or increase or decrease the amount of green chiles in Guacamole—it's up to you. A sure way to please a range of palates is to serve fiery salsa on the side, so guests can heat up their own servings as they choose.

For a party, offer several different appetizers—some cold, some hot. You might also try serving the main course in one room and the appetizers in another. In good weather, start out on the deck or patio; in bad, cozy up to a warm fire.

Hot to Trot Tarts

6 (10- to 12-inch) flour tortillas, cut in quarters
¾ pound chorizo or 1 (15-ounce) can refried pinto or black beans (see Note)
6 eggs or equivalent egg substitute
1 (12-ounce) can evaporated milk
1 ½ tablespoons chopped fresh cilantro
1 teaspoon ground pure New Mexico hot red chile
¾ teaspoon salt
1 ½ cups grated Monterey Jack cheese or low-fat cottage cheese
1 small red onion, very thinly sliced and separated into rings
12 fresh jalapeño or serrano chiles, seeded and cut lengthwise into 8 thin strips

Note: To give the refried beans added flavor, spray a skillet with nonstick cooking spray. Add 2 minced cloves garlic, and cook over low heat until garlic starts to brown. Add beans and 2 tablespoons of minced onion. Stir to combine and heat through.

Fun to make and fun to serve, these spicy yet subtly-flavored tartlets make great party appetizers. You can bake them ahead, and then refrigerate or freeze them.

Preheat the oven to 375°F. Spray each of 24 muffin cups, rather generously, with nonstick cooking spray. Spray the tortilla quarters on both sides, and then place a tortilla quarter in each cup. Bake for 10 minutes, or until the edges are slightly golden. Remove from oven.

Meanwhile, if using chorizo, remove the casings. Cut chorizo into ½-inch slices and fry in a skillet until well browned. Drain well, and set aside. In a bowl, whisk eggs until blended. Whisk in milk, cilantro, ground chile, and salt until well blended. Set aside.

Evenly divide chorizo or beans among tortilla-lined cups. Top evenly with egg mixture, and then with cheese and onion rings. Place 4 chile strips on each tart with tips together in the center and strips radiating out to edges. Set tarts on center rack of oven and bake 15 to 20 minutes, or until egg mixture is firm. Makes 2 dozen tarts

Chile-Cheese Surprises

2 cups grated sharp Cheddar cheese
¼ cup unsalted butter, room temperature
2 tablespoons ground pure New Mexico hot red chile
½ teaspoon salt, if desired
2 tablespoons seeded, de-ribbed, finely minced jalapeño chiles, or to taste
1 cup all-purpose flour
2 tablespoons milk
12 pimento-stuffed green olives
12 pecan halves
12 medium, cooked shrimp, shelled, deveined, and tails removed

Make these tasty treats as feisty or as tame as you like. The rosy cheese pastry flecked with confetti dots of green chile surrounds olives, nuts, and shrimp, making festive-looking treats that are great for holiday get-togethers or any other time of the year. They freeze well, too.

To prepare pastry, combine cheese, butter, and ground chile. Taste, and add salt, if desired. Work in minced jalapeños until evenly distributed. Mix in flour and milk.
Preheat oven to 400°F. Roll out pastry about ⅛-inch thick. Cut pastry into squares, rectangles, or triangles big enough to fit around olives, pecan halves, and shrimp. Place fillings on each pastry piece, and fold pastry over the fillings. Place on ungreased baking sheets and bake 10 to 12 minutes, or until pastry feels firm when pressed.
Makes 3 dozen appetizers

Molded Dome of Cauliflower

A snowy white dome of cauliflower makes a perfect base for a slather of snappy salsa. Guests just pluck off the tender, saucy florets one by one, making this an ideal choice for a cocktail party.

With a sharp knife, cut leaves and stem from cauliflower. Divide cauliflower into florets about 1 ½ inches in diameter. Drop florets into boiling salted water, and boil for about 12 minutes, or until tender when pierced. Drain florets and rinse well under cold running water to stop cooking process. Press a layer of florets, stems in, onto sides and bottom of a 1-quart bowl. Pack center of bowl with more florets, stems up, until all florets have been used. Place a plate and a 1-pound weight (such as canned goods) on packed cauliflower. Let stand for 15 minutes. Then, holding plate and weight in place, tip bowl to drain off water. Refrigerate weighted cauliflower for at least 2 hours.

Remove weight and plate, invert a serving dish over bowl, and then invert bowl and dish together. Lift off bowl and garnish dish with lettuce leaves.

In a separate bowl, whisk together oil, lime juice, salsa, salt, and cayenne. Stir in capers, parsley, watercress, olives, and bell pepper. Spoon some of the sauce over cauliflower. Place remaining sauce in a bowl and set alongside cauliflower. Once the outer layer has been eaten, guests can dunk florets in the sauce in the bowl. ⊰ Makes 4 to 6 servings

1 medium, perfectly-shaped head cauliflower

6 to 8 leaves green or red leaf lettuce

½ cup extra virgin olive oil (see Note)

¼ cup fresh lime juice

¼ cup hot salsa, such Margarita Jalapeño Salsa (see page 128)

¾ teaspoon salt

½ teaspoon cayenne pepper

2 tablespoons chopped capers

1 tablespoon chopped fresh parsley

1 small bunch watercress, coarsely chopped

1 cup pitted ripe olives, thinly sliced

1 red bell pepper, parched (see page 6), peeled, seeded, and cut into ½-inch squares

Note: For a lighter version, reduce the amount of olive oil to 2 tablespoons.

Instant Bloody Marias

1 pint cherry tomatoes
½ cup tequila (or more, as needed)
1 (¾- to 1-ounce) package dry Italian or
   bleu cheese salad dressing mix or 1
   tablespoon seasoned salt and/or pepper
1 teaspoon pequín quebrado
1 small head leaf lettuce or 1 small bunch
   watercress, separated into leaves or
   sprigs

This appetizer is really too easy to be so good…and it is always a favorite with guests. I like to serve this dish festively in my most elegant crystal, or, if going with a Mexican theme, I use fine handmade pottery, setting three matching or somewhat similar dishes on a handsome platter.

Rinse tomatoes, and then pierce each with a wooden pick. Place in a single layer in a dish. Pour in enough tequila to make a shallow layer. Let stand for at least 30 minutes at room temperature. Meanwhile, mix the salad dressing mix (or seasoned salt and/or pepper) with the pequín. Place in a small bowl and set aside.

To serve, cover a large platter with lettuce leaves or watercress. Center the platter with a small glass of tequila, a small glass of wooden picks, and the small dish containing salad dressing mix (or seasoned salt and/or pepper). Arrange tomatoes atop greens.

To eat, spear a tomato with a wooden pick, dip in tequila, and then dip lightly in salad dressing mixture.

↠ Makes 8 to 12 servings

Cuatro-Peppered Goat Cheese Log

2 teaspoons whole black peppercorns
2 teaspoons whole white peppercorns
2 teaspoons dried or pickled green
   peppercorns
1 teaspoon caribe (crushed Northern New
   Mexico red chile)
2 tablespoons finely minced flat-leaf parsley
1 (7- to 8-ounce) log Montrachet or other
   similar goat cheese
Plain white crackers, such as Carr's Water
   Crackers

This delicious appetizer is very easy and quick to make, and it is a bit out of the ordinary.

In a spice grinder or blender, grind black, white, and green peppercorns together. Combine with caribe and mix well. Spread pepper mixture on a sheet of waxed paper. On a second sheet of waxed paper, spread parsley in an even layer as long as cheese log.

Roll cheese log in pepper mixture, using all pepper mixture, and taking care to coat cheese uniformly. Then, lightly roll and press log into parsley. If made ahead, wrap in plastic wrap and refrigerate up to 3 days. Serve at room temperature on an attractive board or plate accompanied by crackers.

↠ Makes 8 servings

Crunchy Hot Crab Bites

These little bites are simple to prepare and serve. If you like, use tuna, cooked shrimp, or even deviled ham in place of the crab.

Preheat broiler. Combine crab, lime or lemon juice, lime peel, green onion, parsley, Worcestershire sauce, mustard, and hot-pepper sauce. Taste and adjust seasonings. Brush melted butter on toast rounds and arrange in a single layer in a broiler pan. Top each round with a portion of the crab mixture, and then with 1 ½ teaspoons cheese. Broil until cheese is melted and crab mixture is hot.

⇥ Make 16 appetizers

1 ½ cups crab meat, drained with all bits of shell removed
1 tablespoon fresh lime or lemon juice
½ teaspoon grated lime peel
1 green onion, minced
2 tablespoons minced fresh parsley
1 teaspoon Worcestershire sauce
1 teaspoon hot prepared mustard, or to taste
Several dashes of liquid hot-pepper sauce, or to taste
2 tablespoons unsalted butter, melted
16 Melba toast rounds
½ cup grated Swiss or sharp Cheddar cheese

Fresh Vietnamese Vegetarian Spring Rolls

When I first sampled a version of these several years ago in Vancouver, I was amazed at just how fresh, light, and delicious they were. After working on ideas for the filling and dipping sauce, these little rolls are some of my new favorites.

Combine all filling ingredients, except for the rice paper wrappers, in a large glass, microwave-safe bowl, and steam for three minutes. Taste and adjust seasoning.

To prepare the Orange Chile Dipping Sauce, combine all sauce ingredients in a medium bowl, and adjust seasoning to taste. Set aside.

Steam the rice wrappers in a plastic bag in the microwave. Create each spring roll by laying a rice paper on a serving plate. Top with filling, placing it closer to one end. Fold each side over to form a flute. Press firmly together. Cover with cellophane wrap and steam in the microwave for about 30 seconds each. Serve with dipping sauce.

⇥ Makes 12 spring rolls

FILLING
4 cups thinly sliced Napa cabbage
1 carrot, julienned
1 cup julienned mushrooms
½ cup julienned red bell pepper
½ cup finely chopped fresh mint
¼ cup coarsely chopped fresh cilantro
1 tablespoon minced fresh ginger
1 tablespoon minced jalapeño chile
1 clove garlic, minced
1 tablespoon mirin
Salt and pepper, to taste
12 (8-inch) rice paper wrappers

ORANGE CHILE DIPPING SAUCE
½ cup orange marmalade
1 tablespoon soy sauce
½ cup rice wine vinegar
1 teaspoon pequín quebrado
1 teaspoon minced fresh ginger
1 clove garlic, minced

Cold & Hot Cucumber Canapés

1 cucumber, about 2 inches in diameter
and 5 to 6 inches long

Kosher or sea salt

1 (3 ⅔-ounce) can smoked oysters, drained

1 teaspoon fresh lime juice, or to taste

2 tablespoons mayonnaise

1 teaspoon dry mustard, or to taste

Several drops of liquid hot-pepper sauce,
or to taste

7 thin slices firm-textured white bread

Mayonnaise

2 teaspoons ground pure New Mexico hot
red chile

Very unusual! Few guests will guess what these canapés are made of until they've taken several bites. I particularly like serving this appetizer in warm weather, but they're terrific any time.

Slice ends from cucumber, and then score sides with the tines of a fork. Cut 28 perfect, very thin crosswise slices from cucumber. Set remaining cucumber aside.

Sprinkle a large, flat, paper-towel-lined plate generously with salt. Carefully place cucumber slices in a single layer on salt. Sprinkle tops of slices with salt and cover with another layer of paper towels. Weigh down with a plate and let stand for about 2 hours at room temperature. Rinse slices and pat dry.

In a food processor or blender, combine oysters, lime juice, 2 tablespoons mayonnaise, mustard, hot-pepper sauce, and remaining cucumber (cut in chunks). Process until well chopped but not puréed. Taste and adjust seasonings. (The mixture can be made as hot as you can handle it.)

Using a biscuit or cookie cutter, cut 28 small rounds of bread; or, if lacking a cutter or short on time, quarter each slice of bread. Spread each round or quarter with mayonnaise, and then with smoked oyster mixture.

Cut each salted cucumber slice almost in half, leaving halves attached just by the rind with a bit of cucumber next to it. Roll each half around your index finger, curling 1 half forward and the other half backward. Set a curled cucumber slice on top of each canapé. Sprinkle canapés with ground chile. ⊰ Makes 28 appetizers

Chile con Queso

This recipe is my very favorite formula for this traditional, cheese-fondue-like dip. I was commissioned to develop the recipe for a major chain of fast-food Mexican restaurants. It keeps in the freezer for 6 months and doubles as a great sauce for vegetables and eggs. Consult the recipes for Chile-Cheese Onions (see page 117) and Sombrero Jalapa (see page 48) for more ideas.

Heat oil in a heavy saucepan, fondue pot, or chafing dish. Add onion and garlic and cook until onion is clear. Stir in flour. Gradually stir in evaporated milk and cook until mixture is thickened. Stir in tomatoes, cheeses, and jalapeños. Cook, stirring, for about 5 minutes, or until cheeses are melted and flavors are well blended. Taste and adjust hotness.

⊰ Makes 2 cups

⅓ cup soybean oil (other vegetable oils don't work as well)
½ cup finely chopped onion
1 clove garlic, minced
1 tablespoon all-purpose flour
¾ cup evaporated milk
¾ cup chopped red-ripe tomato
1 pound processed American cheese, cut in cubes
¼ cup grated sharp Cheddar cheese
¼ cup grated Monterey Jack cheese
¼ cup finely minced jalapeño chiles with juice, or to taste

Spicy Sicilian Cheese Crisps

These terrific-tasting, cheesy bites are good as appetizers, croutons, or special garnishments for small plates. Or, they can be fashioned into taco shells to hold a fresh salad.

Heat oven to 350°F. Mix all ingredients in a bowl. Line a baking sheet with foil and coat with nonstick cooking spray. For large crisps, place ¼ cup cheese mixture onto the baking sheet and spread to form a circle. Repeat with remaining mixture. Bake for 8 to 10 minutes, or until lightly browned. Lift crisps onto a rack to cool or place crisps over a rolling pin to curve into a taco shell. When cooled, stuff taco crisps with favorite salad mixture or serve flat alongside or mixed into a fresh garden salad.

⊰ Makes 6 large or 12 small crisps

6 ounces shredded Italian cheese blend
1 tablespoon cornmeal
½ cup finely chopped piñon nuts
½ teaspoon pequín quebrado

Guacamole

2 ripe Hass avocados (see Note)
¼ cup chopped tomato
Juice of ½ lime
¼ cup finely chopped onion
1 clove garlic, finely minced
1 medium fresh jalapeño chile, finely
   minced
¾ teaspoon salt, or to taste

*Note: Avocados vary greatly in size and flavor.
This recipe calls for medium-sized avocados. If
using smaller avocados, always add a portion of the
tomato and onion and sample before serving.*

Everyone likes guacamole—a lively avocado dip that can double as a salad or topping. In addition to serving it the traditional way with warm tortilla chips, I use it as a topping or filling for a variety of dishes such as burgers, pork chops, omelets, and tacos.

Halve and pit avocados and scoop flesh into a bowl. Using 2 knives, cut flesh into ½-inch cubes. Add tomato, lime juice, onion, garlic, jalapeño, and salt. Lightly toss together. Taste and adjust seasonings. Serve immediately.

ᵊ Makes 4 to 6 servings

Brennan's Clams

24 cherrystone or other small clams
2 tablespoons cornmeal or fine dry bread
   crumbs
½ cup unsalted butter or Hot Pepper
   Butter (see page 124)
½ lemon, cut in 2 wedges
Very Hot Shrimp Cocktail Sauce (see
   page 126)

*Note: Discard any clams that don't open—
do NOT eat them!*

These clams are so much fun, and they're so easy to make. I'm sure they'll become a favorite appetizer whenever you are barbecuing!

Thoroughly rinse clams, and then place in a single layer on a baking pan. Add water to a depth of 3 inches, and sprinkle on cornmeal or crumbs. Let soak at least 30 minutes so clams will exchange the sand inside their shells for the cornmeal or crumbs.

Meanwhile, ignite coals in a barbecue grill. Melt butter or Hot Pepper Butter in a saucepan. Squeeze lemon wedges into butter and keep warm.

To cook clams, place directly on hot coals 3 or 4 at a time. Cook just until shells pop open (see Note). To eat, remove clams from shells with a fork. Dip clams in lemon butter, and then in Very Hot Shrimp Cocktail Sauce.

ᵊ Makes 2 dozen clams

Fluffy Greek Cheese-Chile Pastries

Inspired by the popular Greek appetizers, these melt-in-your-mouth delicacies, spruced up with zesty green chiles, are guaranteed to please almost everyone. Be prepared to make a lot of these tasty pastries! The filo pastry keeps well in the freezer, so the prepared appetizers, either baked or unbaked, can be frozen for up to 3 months. (To bake frozen pastries, increase baking time by about 15 minutes.)

Preheat oven to 350°F. Brush baking sheets with melted butter. Beat eggs, cheeses, parsley, and salt together until well blended. Set aside.

Stack 2 pastry sheets. Cut stacked sheets lengthwise into 3-inch-wide strips. Brush each 2-layer strip with melted butter on both sides, and then place a spoonful of cheese filling at 1 end of each strip. Top with a few pieces of chile. Fold 1 corner of strip over filling to create a triangular end, and then fold triangle over on itself. Continue to fold triangle from side to side until you reach end of pastry strip—you should have a triangle-shaped pastry. Pierce top of pastry with a wooden pick and place on buttered baking sheet. Continue making pastries with remaining ingredients. Bake for 30 to 40 minutes, or until golden and flaky.

🖙 Makes about 4 dozen pastries

2 tablespoons melted unsalted butter (see Note)
2 eggs
2 cups small-curd cottage cheese
1 pound crumbled feta cheese (see Tip)
¼ cup chopped fresh parsley
Pinch of salt
8 to 12 ounces filo pastry (strudel leaves), thawed if frozen
½ cup canned diced green chiles or ½ cup fresh New Mexico hot green chiles, parched (see page 6), peeled, seeded, and chopped

Note: To reduce calories, use nonstick cooking spray to brush the baking sheets and to spray the pastry. The flavor will not be as rich, but there will be far less fat and calories.

Tip: If you prefer a milder flavor cheese, substitute Munster for the feta.

Quesadillas

2 tablespoons sweet unsalted butter or
   nonstick cooking spray
6 (9- to 10-inch) flour tortillas
1 cup grated Monterey Jack cheese
¼ cup thinly sliced fresh or pickled
   jalapeño chiles, or to taste
Favorite filling such as cooked chorizo,
   chicken, beef, baby shrimp, or refried
   beans
6 small leaves red leaf lettuce (see Tip)
Guacamole or sour cream
1 red-ripe tomato, diced
Caribe (crushed Northern New Mexico
   red chile), if desired

*Tip: For a simple variation on the presentation,
place a spoonful of salsa in the center of the plate
and spread evenly. Place the quesadilla pieces over
it, allowing the salsa to extend out across the entire
plate. Omit the lettuce, sour cream or Guacamole,
tomato, and caribe.*

Simple to prepare, quesadillas are traditionally made from flour tortillas filled with Monterey Jack cheese and fresh jalapeños. But other fillings are equally good—try any taco filling or any mixture of meats, chiles, sour cream, and cheeses. Add a dollop of homemade Guacamole (see page 15) to the side of each serving.

Place a comal (Spanish for flat griddle) over medium-high heat and lightly brush griddle with butter in a half moon—the shape of half the size of the tortilla—or spray with non-stick cooking spray. Place 1 tortilla on the buttered area. Sprinkle a layer of cheese over half the tortilla, allowing a 1-inch margin. Add the jalapeño pieces and a little of the favorite filling, if using. Fold unused side of tortilla over the buttered side. Let cook until bottom is golden. Brush the top of the folded tortilla with butter or spray with nonstick cooking spray and flip carefully onto the hot surface. Cook second side until golden, and then remove to a cutting board.

Slice each quesadilla into triangular quarters or sixths and place on a plate with the points facing the center of the plate. Tuck a leaf of lettuce under the center of each point. Place a dollop of Guacamole or sour cream on the lettuce in the center where all the points come together. Dot with tomato pieces and a little caribe, if desired.

Makes 1 ½ dozen appetizers

Red Pepper Baskets with Crudités & Rosy Creamy Salsa

Grand enough to kick off a multi-course meal, this pretty appetizer is a lovely choice for any outdoor party. If you wish, group the baskets together on a lettuce-lined platter for a buffet table.

Slice stem ends from bell peppers, and pull out seeds and ribs. Divide broccoli into florets with stems about 4 inches long. Cut tips from green beans. Trim asparagus spears to 6-inches long, and pare skin from stalks. Pull strings from snow peas. Parboil each vegetable, except for the red bell peppers, separately in boiling salted water just until tender-crisp. Broccoli, green beans, and asparagus each take about 3 minutes; snow peas take about 30 seconds. When each vegetable is done, transfer it to an ice-filled dish to cool.

While vegetables are cooling, combine sour cream, mayonnaise, and salsa in a medium bowl. Spoon ¼ of the mixture into each pepper cup (see Note). Stand broccoli, green beans, asparagus, and snow peas in pepper cups and serve. ⤙ Make 4 servings

4 red bell peppers
1 bunch fresh broccoli
⅓ pound fresh green beans
12 small fresh asparagus spears
¼ pound fresh snow peas
½ cup dairy sour cream
½ cup mayonnaise
⅓ cup Margarita Jalapeño Salsa (see page 128) or other hot red salsa

Note: You can also serve this appetizer with a separate red bell pepper boat filled with the salsa mixture instead of placing the salsa mixture in the bottom of the cup.

Exciting Escargots

The sassy flavors of caribe and Margarita Jalapeño Salsa make for a brand new version of this always-elegant appetizer. Serve in small ovenproof earthenware casserole dishes.

Preheat oven to 425°F. Melt butter in a skillet, add garlic, and sauté until garlic barely begins to turn golden. Place 6 escargots in each of 6 individual casserole dishes. Drizzle evenly with garlic butter. Spoon 2 heaping tablespoons of salsa evenly over escargots in each dish. Sprinkle 1 teaspoon of caribe over each. Bake for 15 to 20 minutes, or until the sauce sizzles.

Meanwhile, warm tortillas or slice and warm French bread. Serve escargots with tortillas or bread for dunking. ⤙ Makes 6 servings

1 cup unsalted butter (see Note)
3 tablespoons minced garlic
36 large, canned escargots
1 cup Margarita Jalapeño Salsa (see page 128)
2 tablespoons caribe (crushed Northern New Mexico red chile)
12 (6-inch) flour or corn tortillas or 1 small loaf French bread

Note: For fewer calories, you can reduce the butter by half or use a lower-calorie substitute such as reduced-fat margarine.

*Red Pepper Baskets with
Crudités & Rosy Creamy Salsa*

Zappo Avocado Appetizers

So delightfully flavorful! The creaminess of the avocado contrasts with the crunchy corn batter and smooth chile-cheese filling, making a very special and unusual appetizer.

Halve, pit, and carefully peel avocados. Place strips of jalapeño in each avocado cavity, and then pack cavities with cheeses. In a deep, heavy saucepan, heat 2 to 3 inches of oil to 375°F. Then, in a bowl, stir together flour, baking powder, salt, and cornmeal. Beat in milk and eggs until blended. Dip each filled avocado half (see Note) into batter to coat completely. Fry in hot oil until golden brown. Serve hot with a side dish of salsa. ⊰ Makes 4 servings

2 avocados
1 large fresh jalapeño chile, cut into thin strips
¼ cup coarsely grated Monterey Jack cheese
¼ cup coarsely grated Cheddar cheese
Vegetable oil
1 cup all-purpose flour
1 teaspoon baking powder
½ teaspoon salt
¾ cup cornmeal
1 cup milk
2 eggs, slightly beaten
Margarita Jalapeño Salsa (see page 128) or other hot or mild salsa

Note: If desired, slice the filled avocado into 1-inch-thick slivers before dipping in batter and frying. The smaller pieces will make it somewhat easier to eat.

Oyster Hot Shots

Tuck these peppy, luxuriously sauced oysters back in their shells after baking (or bake them in the shells, if you wish—just place them on a bed of rock salt in a baking pan). If you prefer, you can serve them on toast rounds or in tortilla shells. Or, for a regal first course or light main dish, serve the oysters in scallop shells surrounded by a border of mashed potatoes.

Preheat oven to 375°F. Using some of the butter, generously butter a 9-inch-square baking pan. Place oysters in pan and set aside.

In a medium, heavy saucepan, combine wine, lime juice, garlic, and onion. When mixture just begins to bubble, reduce heat and simmer gently, uncovered, until mixture is reduced to about ¼ of its original volume. Whisk in cream and remaining butter until butter is completely incorporated. Taste and adjust seasonings. Spoon sauce over oysters and bake about 6 minutes, or until edges of oysters just begin to curl. Spoon each oyster into a half-shell, and then decorate with jalapeño slices and a sprinkle of caribe. Serve immediately, or keep hot in a warm oven or on a warming tray until ready to serve. ⊰ Make 16 appetizers

⅓ cup unsalted butter, room temperature
16 medium, fresh oysters, shucked (reserve oyster shells)
1 cup dry white wine
½ cup fresh lime juice
1 tablespoon minced garlic
3 tablespoons finely minced onion
⅓ cup whipping cream
4 to 6 fresh jalapeño chiles, cut crosswise in very thin slices and seeded
1 teaspoon caribe (crushed Northern New Mexico red chile)

Lebanese Grape Leaf Rolls

1 (12- to 16-ounce) jar grape leaves or
   3 dozen small or 2 dozen large fresh
   leaves, wilted
2 lamb bones
3 cloves garlic
1 pound ground lamb
½ cup uncooked long-grain white rice
½ teaspoon ground cinnamon
1 teaspoon salt
½ teaspoon freshly ground black pepper
1 tablespoon caribe (crushed Northern
   New Mexico red chile)
Juice of 1 lemon
¼ cup sugar
1 (28-ounce) can whole tomatoes

In Albuquerque, I planted a whole vineyard just to harvest the leaves for this dish! If you're lucky enough to have fresh grape leaves at hand, just pick new leaves that are still thin and tender and then wilt them briefly in a steamer. Use the prepared leaves immediately or freeze them flat with plastic wrap between the layers in an airtight, moisture-proof container.

These rolls are wonderful when served with Greek avgolemono sauce, spicy aromatic tomato sauce, or a sweet-hot sauce such as the one below. Make the rolls small for appetizers or larger for an entrée.

Rinse grape leaves. If necessary, soak bottled or fresh leaves in hot water just until pliable. Place lamb bones and garlic in bottom of a large saucepan. In a medium bowl, mix ground lamb, rice, cinnamon, salt, pepper, caribe, lemon juice, and sugar. Place a spoonful of lamb mixture on each leaf and roll up, tucking ends in. Place rolled leaves on top of bones in pan. Drain liquid from canned tomatoes into pan. Coarsely chop remaining tomatoes and add to pan. Add enough water to come just below tops of rolls. Bring mixture to a boil over high heat. Reduce heat, cover, and simmer about 30 minutes, or until rice in filling is tender. Serve immediately. ✠ Makes 3 dozen small or 2 dozen large rolls

Picante Pesto-Topped Oysters on the Half-Shell

These juicy oysters are topped with a fiery version of the familiar Italian pesto sauce, but chiles, not the traditional basil, make the pesto base. Select the heat of chiles you prefer, keeping in mind that oysters are quite bland and off-set spicy toppings perfectly.

Preheat oven to 400°F. In a food processor or blender, combine all but 2 tablespoons of the Romano cheese, the green and red chiles, garlic, nuts, Parmesan cheese, cilantro, and nutmeg. Process until puréed. With motor running, add butter in a thin stream, processing until well blended.

Line 4 pie plates or rimmed ovenproof plates with rock salt. Place 4 oysters on top of the salt on each plate, and top each oyster with a spoonful of chile pesto. Bake for 6 to 8 minutes, or until pesto is bubbly. Remove oysters from oven, and sprinkle evenly with reserved 2 tablespoons Romano cheese. Broil just until cheese is melted. Garnish each serving with 3 lime wedges and a sprinkling of caribe.

⇥ Makes 4 servings

⅓ cup freshly grated Romano cheese

3 large fresh green chiles (as hot as you like), parched (see page 6), peeled, and seeded

2 dried Chinese hot red chiles

4 cloves garlic

¼ cup piñon nuts

3 tablespoons freshly grated Parmesan cheese

3 tablespoons chopped fresh cilantro

Freshly grated nutmeg, to taste

½ cup unsalted butter, melted (see Note)

2 to 3 cups rock salt

16 large fresh oysters on the half-shell

2 limes, cut lengthwise in 6 wedges

2 teaspoons caribe (crushed Northern New Mexico red chile)

Note: To lower the calorie and fat intake, you can reduce the butter to ¼ cup without sacrificing flavor.

Picante Pesto-Topped Oysters on the Half-Shell

Soups and Salads

Turn up the Heat

BUBBLE, BUBBLE—BUBBLE AND BREW... A steaming pot of soup satisfies like nothing else. Most of the soups in this chapter are sizzling-hot and spicy. As always, though, you can adjust the amount of chiles and spices to suit your palate. And, if you're looking for a real break from the heat, try the Soothing Leek Soup. Mild, creamy, and perfect for a light luncheon entrée, it's also a great beginning for a spicy-hot meal.

   The salads in these pages are good partners for soup, and creative seasoning makes all of them distinctly out of the ordinary. Holiday Salad of Peppers and Endive is refreshingly crisp and snappy with its salsa vinaigrette; minted Tropical Fruit Salad is cool, sweet, and soothing; and sassy Acapulco Salad offers a sure-fire way to brighten any meal.

Brazilian Black Bean Soup

2 cups dried black beans

8 cups cold water

¾ pound cooked ham, diced

1 ham bone, if desired

4 cloves garlic, crushed

2 teaspoons salt

½ cup diced onion

2 whole cloves

½ teaspoon ground cumin, or to taste

1 tablespoon caribe (crushed Northern New Mexico red chile), or to taste

Juice of 1 lime

¼ cup rum

4 green onions, finely chopped

½ cup grated Monterey Jack cheese or dairy sour cream

Lime wedges, if desired

Make this soup as feisty as you like—it's easy to temper the heat by adjusting the amount of chiles. A topping of cheese or sour cream and a float of rum help soothe the fire of the brew. Serve this soup as a first course or as a light entrée.

Sort and rinse beans, and then soak overnight in water to cover. (Or place beans in a large saucepan and add water to cover. Bring to a boil. Remove from heat, cover, and let stand 1 hour. Return to heat and simmer 1 ½ hours. Proceed with recipe.)

Drain beans and place in a large saucepan. Add 8 cups cold water, ham, ham bone, if desired, garlic, salt, diced onion, cloves, cumin, caribe, and lime juice. Bring to a boil, reduce heat, cover, and simmer for 2 hours, or until beans are tender and soup is thick. Taste and adjust seasonings.

To serve, remove ham bone, if used. Lace soup with rum, spoon into bowls, and top with green onions, cheese or sour cream, and lime wedges, if desired.

Makes 4 to 6 servings

Hot Garlic Sopa

1 or 2 tablespoons olive oil

4 large cloves garlic, minced

4 (6-inch) corn tortillas, cut in 6 pieces or 1 cup tortilla chips

4 cups beef broth

1 or 2 fresh New Mexico hot green chiles, parched (see page 6), peeled, seeded, and chopped

About 1 teaspoon ground pure New Mexico hot red chile

2 (6-inch) corn tortillas, cut into ¼-inch strips and fried until crisp

½ cup grated Monterey Jack cheese

4 slices fresh or pickled jalapeño

Note: For a main dish soup, add a poached egg to each soup bowl before adding the soup and toppings.

This is one of my Uncle Harry's favorite soups—a delightful dish he learned to make while living in Mexico. Serve it as hot as you can handle it!

Heat oil (use only 1 tablespoon oil if using tortilla chips) in a 3-quart saucepan with a close-fitting lid. Add garlic and cook briefly. Add tortilla pieces or chips and cook until lightly browned, crushing chips with the back of a wooden spoon. Stir in broth, green chiles, and 1 teaspoon of the ground chile. Bring to a simmer.

Meanwhile, preheat oven to 450°F. Taste soup and adjust seasoning, adding ground pure hot chile powder to taste. Set 4 ovenproof bowls on a baking sheet (see Note). Evenly divide the soup between the bowls. Top each serving with ¼ of the extra, fried tortilla strips, ¼ of the cheese, and a jalapeño slice. Place in the oven until the cheese melts and then serve hot. Makes 4 servings

Chipotle Corn Chowder

When Tamara first made this soup and was so proud of it, she brought some to work. I really liked it! The smokiness of the chipotles pairs nicely with the corn and cream. Serve this chowder warm.

Preheat grill or use broiler. Lightly brush the ears of corn and onion with oil. Place on grill or under broiler and grill until brown flecks appear on each.

Meanwhile, reconstitute chipotles with a splash of vinegar (cider vinegar is best) and water to cover. In a microwave, place chiles in bottom of a 1-quart glass measuring cup, cover, and cook on high for five minutes, or for the stovetop, cover and simmer for 30 minutes. Set aside.

Cut corn off cob, reserving ¼ cup for garnish, and coarsely chop onion. Place one cup water in blender jar, add corn and onion, and process until puréed. Add chipotle chiles and process further. Place mixture in saucepan, add heavy cream, pepper, and cumin and simmer for about 15 minutes. While chowder is simmering, prepare topping by combining reserved grilled corn, green bell pepper, red bell pepper, jalapeño, vinegar, and honey. Taste and add salt, if desired. Ladle soup into individual bowls, top with a spoonful of topping, and serve immediately. ⇥ Makes 4 servings

6 ears yellow or white corn
½ onion
1 teaspoon olive oil
2 to 3 dried chipotles
1 cup water
4 cups heavy cream
½ teaspoon freshly ground pepper, preferably white
½ teaspoon ground cumin

SOUP TOPPING
¼ cup grilled corn reserved from above
½ tablespoon chopped green bell pepper
½ tablespoon chopped red bell pepper
½ fresh jalapeño, minced
3 tablespoons white wine vinegar
1 teaspoon honey
Salt, if desired

Speedy Salsa-Dressed Potato Salad

When you want a different twist on the same old potato salad, try this one. It is a good choice for picnicking, because it does not contain mayonnaise. The flavor improves with at least 2 hours of marinating, or it can even be made a day ahead. Serve at room temperature.

Bring a quart of water to boil in a medium saucepan, adding salt. When boiling, add the potatoes and cook until tender, about 15 minutes. Drain well. Meanwhile, in a small bowl, combine salsa, lime juice, oil, and pepper. Add sauce to cooked potatoes, and mix well. Stir in tomatoes, olives, green onions, and cilantro. Toss to coat, and serve immediately. ⇥ Makes 4 servings

¼ teaspoon salt, or to taste
1 pound small red or waxy new potatoes, cut into 1-inch pieces
¼ cup Sonoran-Style Chipotle Tomatillo Salsa (see page 127)
1 to 2 tablespoons lime juice
1 tablespoon olive oil
⅛ teaspoon freshly ground black pepper
1 large tomato, seeded and chopped
½ cup sliced ripe olives
¼ cup sliced green onions
1 tablespoon coarsely chopped cilantro

Chipotle Corn Chowder

Cream of Broccoli Soup, Caliente

So smooth and flavorful, this basic soup is versatile, too—it can be made with almost any green vegetable (you might try asparagus, spinach, Swiss chard, or zucchini). The caliente character comes from fresh green chiles; use one or more to make the soup as tame or zesty as you wish.

For the best, most special flavor in this and other soups, use homemade chicken broth. After stewing a chicken, store the broth in the freezer until you're ready to cook another bird. Then use it again, adding extra flavor with vegetables and herbs…and then freeze again until the next use.

Place broth in a medium, heavy saucepan. Add broccoli, cover, and bring to a simmer.

Meanwhile, melt butter in a small skillet. Add onion and cook until lightly browned. Add onion mixture to broccoli-broth mixture, cover, and simmer about 30 minutes, or until onion is very soft. While mixture is still hot, process in a food processor or blender until smoothly puréed. Add jalapeño or serrano chiles, taste, and adjust seasonings, adding salt to taste. Return soup to pan and place over very low heat.

In a separate bowl, beat cream and egg yolks together. Pour into soup in a very thin stream, stirring constantly. Cook, stirring, until soup coats a wooden spoon in a fine film. Do not let soup boil or it may curdle. Immediately pour soup into soup cups, sprinkle with caribe, and serve piping hot. ⊰ Makes 4 servings

2 cups double-strength chicken broth
1 cup chopped fresh broccoli or frozen chopped broccoli, thawed and drained
2 tablespoons unsalted butter
1 medium onion, coarsely chopped
1 or more fresh jalapeño or serrano chiles, finely minced
Salt, to taste
1 cup whipping cream (see Note)
2 egg yolks
1 tablespoon caribe (crushed Northern New Mexico red chile), or to taste

Note: For less fat and calories, substitute 1 cup of evaporated skim milk for the whipping cream.

Szechwan Hot and Sour Soup

6 dried cloud ear mushrooms

6 dried Chinese black mushrooms

6 dried tigerlily buds

4 ½ cups double-strength chicken broth

1 tablespoon peanut oil

1 tablespoon sesame oil

About 1 tablespoon light soy sauce

⅓ pound lean, boneless pork or skinned, boned chicken breast, cut in long, thin strips

1 (4-ounce) cake fresh bean curd, cut in thin strips

¼ cup bamboo shoots, cut in thin strips

2 eggs, slightly beaten

2 tablespoons Chinese red rice vinegar

2 tablespoons thinly sliced green onion (including some green top)

2 teaspoons sesame oil

1 teaspoon freshly ground white pepper, Hot Hot Oil (see page 123), or chile oil

Sugar, if desired

This very popular spicy-yet-sour soup is a wonderful warm-up on cold days, especially after an afternoon of skiing or skating. As a first course, it's a terrific starter for any Oriental menu. Look for the tigerlily buds and dried mushrooms in Asian markets and well-stocked supermarkets.

Pour boiling water over cloud ears, black mushrooms, and tigerlily buds. Let soak 15 minutes. Drain, and cut off woody parts of mushrooms and hard tips of buds. Slice mushrooms and buds very thinly. Set aside.

Heat broth in a large saucepan. Meanwhile, heat peanut oil and 1 tablespoon sesame oil in a wok or large skillet. When oil is hot, sprinkle on 1 tablespoon soy sauce. Add pork or chicken and stir-fry just a few minutes, or until crisp on edges. Add sliced mushrooms and tigerlily buds and stir to brown edges lightly. Add meat-mushroom mixture to heated broth and stir well. Stir in bean curd and bamboo shoots. When soup comes to a gentle simmer, pour in beaten eggs, stirring soup with a swirling motion. As soon as eggs start to cook, remove soup from heat.

Rinse 4 to 6 individual soup bowls or 1 large serving bowl with hot water. In a separate bowl, mix vinegar, green onion, 2 teaspoons sesame oil, and white pepper, Hot Hot Oil, or chile oil. Divide mixture equally among sauce or perhaps a pinch of sugar if a less sour flavor is desired. Stir to mix the cloudlike shreds of egg evenly, then pour into individual bowls or serving bowl. To eat, bring soup spoon up from the bottom of bowl to mix hot and sour flavors into each bite. ⊰ Makes 4 to 6 servings.

Soothing Leek Soup

Because this smooth soup is not hot, it's a comforting starter to serve before very hot entrées. When you want a change from spicy fare, perhaps you'll enjoy this as much as I do.

Melt butter in a heavy saucepan. Add onion and leek and cook slowly, stirring often, until soft. Stir in broth, and then add potato. Cover and cook until potato is tender. Allow to cool. Add cooled leek mixture to a food processor or blender and process until puréed. Set aside.

In another saucepan, bring cream to a gentle simmer. Cook until slightly reduced, stir in leek mixture, and heat until very hot (do no boil). Season with salt, pepper, and nutmeg. To serve, spoon into individual bowls, sprinkle 1 tablespoon cheese over each serving, and offer a shot of wine on the side. ⊰ Makes 4 servings

2 tablespoons unsalted butter

2 tablespoons finely chopped onion

1 large leek, rinsed very well and sliced crosswise

2 cups double-strength chicken broth

1 cup diced peeled potato

1 ½ cups whipping cream (see Note)

¾ teaspoon salt, or to taste

Freshly ground black pepper, to taste

Freshly grated nutmeg, to taste

¼ cup crumbled bleu cheese or freshly grated Parmesan cheese

4 shots dry white wine

Note: For less fat and calories, substitute the same amount of evaporated skim milk for the whipping cream. Also, to further reduce the fat, use less cheese for each serving.

Mexican Papas Sopa

Traditionally only moderately spicy, this hearty soup is substantial enough to serve as a light lunch or supper, and smaller servings make a nice first course for a light meal. If you enjoy fiery flavors, just include more chiles—the addition of seven or eight will really turn up the heat!

Brown salt pork or heat oil in a large, heavy, flat-bottomed pot. Add potatoes and cook until browned. Add onion and cook until clear. Stir in broth and jalapeños. Bring to a boil, reduce heat, cover, and simmer 1 hour, or until potatoes are very soft. Remove salt pork cubes, if using. Taste and add salt and more chiles as desired.

To serve, preheat broiler. Set 4 to 6 heated soup bowls on a baking sheet. Spoon soup into bowls, and top each serving with a circle of cheese centered with a sprinkle of caribe. Broil just until cheese is bubbly, and then serve warm. ⊰ Makes 4 to 6 servings

¼ pound salt pork, cut in 1-inch cubes or 2 tablespoons vegetable oil

3 large or 4 medium potatoes, peeled and diced

½ cup chopped onion

6 cups chicken broth

2 to 8 fresh jalapeño chiles, finely slivered

Salt, to taste

⅓ pound Monterey Jack cheese, coarsely grated

Caribe (crushed Northern New Mexico red chile)

Great-Grandma's Louisiana Gumbo

¾ pound boneless beef chuck (or use pork shoulder, chicken, or seafood)

2 tablespoons all-purpose flour

2 tablespoons vegetable oil

1 pound fresh okra, cut in 1-inch slices or 1 (12-ounce) package frozen sliced okra, thawed and drained

2 large red-ripe tomatoes, peeled and cut in wedges about ¾-inch thick

2 medium onions, chopped

1 small green bell pepper, cut in large squares

1 large clove garlic, minced

1 teaspoon file powder, or to taste

¾ teaspoon salt, or to taste

Liquid hot pepper sauce, to taste

Hot cooked rice

My Swedish grandmother's mother got this recipe from one of her helpers whose home was in Louisiana. The original recipe was a real kick—it called for a 10-cent soup bone, a sack full of freshly picked okra, and so on—but I tested and retested it with modern measurements, finally achieving the true flavor of Grandma's gumbo. To please those who like their gumbo searing hot as well as those who don't, I recommend seasoning it lightly with hot pepper sauce and then serving additional sauce at the table. File powder, crucial for an authentic flavor, is quite strong-tasting; I have developed the recipe with only a small amount, but those who enjoy the flavor (as I do) can add more to taste. Serve the gumbo over fluffy steamed long-grain rice.

Cut meat in 1-inch cubes, and then dredge in flour. Heat oil in a large, heavy saucepan, add floured meat, and cook until browned. If the meat begins to stick, add a bit more oil. Remove meat from pan, add okra, and cook until browned (browning prevents the okra from taking on the somewhat slimy texture that many find unpleasant). Return meat to pan, and stir in tomatoes, onions, bell pepper, and garlic. Add water to cover. Bring to a boil, reduce heat, cover, and simmer 1 ½ to 2 hours, or until meat is tender and mixture has the consistency of thick soup. Add file powder, salt, and hot-pepper sauce. Simmer 30 minutes longer. Adjust seasonings, and then serve over rice. ⚔ Makes 4 servings

Gail's Caribbean Salad

1 cup fresh-cooked or canned corn kernels

1 cup black beans, drained and rinsed

¼ cup chopped green onions

½ cup diced red bell pepper

½ cup coarsely chopped fresh cilantro

1 tablespoon olive oil

2 teaspoons cider vinegar

½ teaspoon freshly ground black pepper, or to taste

½ teaspoon kosher or sea salt, or to taste

1 teaspoon ground chipotle chile, or to taste

This quick-to-make salad is a great complement to light entrées such as fish, seafood, or poultry—or it is hearty enough for a main dish.

Place corn, black beans, green onions, bell pepper, and cilantro in a large, non-reactive bowl. Stir to combine ingredients. Drizzle with oil and vinegar. Sprinkle with black pepper, salt, and ground chipotle. Toss to coat. Taste, adjust seasonings, and serve immediately. ⚔ Makes 4 servings

Wicked Watercress and Potato Soup

This soup is simple to make, yet elegantly flavored! Though spiced, this soup is kind to the stomach. It's a great first course of light luncheon entrée.

Place broth in a medium saucepan. Add potatoes, onion, and watercress, lettuce, or spinach. Bring to a boil over high heat. Reduce heat to low, cover, and simmer about 20 minutes, or until potatoes are tender. Pour vegetables and some of the broth into a blender or food processor. Process until smoothly puréed and then return to pan. Add salt, white pepper, and milk; heat until steaming. Ladle into soup bowls and sprinkle generously with black pepper.

Makes 4 servings

4 cups chicken broth
2 medium potatoes, peeled and diced
1 tablespoon instant minced onion
1 cup coarsely chopped watercress, leaf lettuce, or fresh spinach
½ teaspoon salt, or to taste
1 teaspoon freshly ground white pepper
1 cup skim milk
Freshly ground black pepper, to taste

Manny's Feisty Kale Soup with Black Beans and Kielbasa

This full flavored, spicy soup is reminiscent of gumbo when served over a bed of fluffy rice with some hot, freshly-made Margarita Jalapeño Salsa (see page 128, omit the tequila from the salsa).

Blacken the tomatoes on a stovetop grill, outdoor grill, or under a broiler. First core and cut an "x" on the bottom of each tomato. Lightly oil each tomato with ½ tablespoon of the oil and grill or broil until blackened. When cool, peel and chop. At the same time, grill the Kielbasa until slightly blackened. Cut into ½-inch rounds. Set aside.

Meanwhile, heat the remaining oil, add the onion and garlic, and sauté until clear. Add the kale, black beans, green chiles, tomatoes, Kielbasa, stock, salt, and 1 teaspoon of the cumin. Simmer for 30 minutes, or until kale is tender. Add remaining cumin just before serving. Serve as a stew or over fluffy rice with a topping of fresh salsa.

Makes 6 to 8 servings

4 fresh tomatoes or 1 (15-ounce) can stewed tomatoes
2 tablespoons olive or vegetable oil
1 pound Kielbasa
1 medium onion, chopped
3 fresh garlic cloves, minced
1 (1-inch diameter) bunch kale, coarsely chopped
2 cups cooked black beans or 1 (15-ounce) can black beans
4 to 6 New Mexico green chiles, parched (see page 6), peeled, and sliced
2 cups vegetable or chicken stock
1 teaspoon salt, or to taste
2 teaspoons cumin

Sauerkraut Soup

2 tablespoons unsalted butter or vegetable oil

1 pound lean, boneless pork, cubed

½ cup chopped lean ham

1 pound lean hot link sausage, halved lengthwise (see Note)

3 onions, coarsely chopped

1 cup dry white wine

3 cups chicken broth

1 (1-pound) can sauerkraut or 1 pound fresh sauerkraut, undrained

1 tablespoon anise seeds

½ teaspoon cayenne pepper, or to taste

¼ cup chopped fresh parsley

¾ cup dairy sour cream

Note: If the hot Bavarian type of sausage is not available, use link breakfast sausage and add an additional ½ teaspoon cayenne pepper to soup. Also, for a lower fat version, substitute 1 pound lean ham for the link sausage.

A close friend of mine, Janet Pugh, lived in Bavaria for many years. While there, she discovered this hearty, sour-hot soup tamed with sour cream.

Melt butter in a large, deep, heavy pot. Add pork cubes and brown evenly. Add the ham and sausage and cook until sausage is browned. Drain off excess fat. Add onions to the same pot and cook until clear. Add wine and stir about 3 minutes, or just long enough to deglaze pan. To the meat and onions, stir in broth, sauerkraut, anise seeds, cayenne, and parsley. Bring to a boil, reduce heat to low, cover, and simmer about 1 ½ hours, or until flavors are well blended and pork is tender. Cut the sausage into bite-size pieces and return to the pot. Spoon soup into large bowls. Offer sour cream on the side. ❧ Makes 6 to 8 servings

Southwestern Vichyssoise

¼ cup butter

4 leeks, white part only, sliced

1 medium onion, sliced

5 medium potatoes, peeled and sliced

1 quart chicken broth

3 cups milk

1 tablespoon salt, or to taste

2 cups half-and-half or heavy cream

7 ounces chopped green chiles

8 ounces extra sharp Cheddar cheese, grated Cheddar cheese, grated, if desired

1 fresh jalapeño chile, thinly sliced, if desired

The combination of green chile and cheese is almost heaven! When added to eggs, chicken, tortillas, rice—the list is almost endless—they are automatically tastier. This great summer soup could also be served hot in colder months.

In a 5-quart saucepan or small stockpot, melt the butter over medium heat. Add the leeks and onion and cook until clear and lightly browned. Add potatoes, broth, milk, and salt, and boil for 35 minutes, or until potatoes are tender. Place mixture in a blender and purée. Return the mixture to the pan and add half-and-half or cream. Add green chiles and cheese and stir well. Spoon into individual servings bowls, and garnish, if desired, with a sprinkle of cheese and a thin slice of jalapeño. ❧ Makes 6 to 8 servings

Caribbean Jerk Chicken Salad

Spicy jerk seasonings were originally created as a preservative for meats. They really spice up your palate and are great paired with greens and vegetables in a nice fresh salad.

Place water, lime juice, rum, allspice, cinnamon, coriander, nutmeg, turmeric, onion, habanero or pequín, and salt in a blender and process until thoroughly combined. Place chicken in a non-reactive, shallow bowl and spread mixture over the chicken in a thick paste. Allow to set for two hours or overnight in the refrigerator.

    Prepare the lettuce and divide among four large plates or shallow bowls. To prepare the dressing, whisk together the oil, mustard, garlic, white vinegar, and sherry vinegar. Set aside.

    Remove chicken from marinade and grill until done, about 4 minutes on each side. Slice each breast into 1-inch-wide strips and artfully place in a radial pattern over the lettuce. Scatter tomatoes equally among the salads. Sprinkle with scallions. Drizzle the dressing over the salads and sprinkle with freshly ground pepper, if desired.
    Makes 4 servings

- 2 tablespoons water
- 2 tablespoons freshly-squeezed lime juice
- 2 tablespoons dark rum
- 1 tablespoon ground allspice
- 1 ½ teaspoons ground cinnamon
- 1 ½ teaspoons ground coriander
- ¾ teaspoon ground nutmeg
- 2 teaspoons ground turmeric
- ½ cup onion, chopped
- 1 fresh habanero chile or 1 teaspoon pequín quebrado
- 1 teaspoon salt
- 2 pounds boneless, skinless chicken breast
- 1 large head Romaine lettuce, rinsed and torn into medium-sized pieces
- 6 tablespoons extra virgin olive oil
- 1 teaspoon Dijon mustard
- 1 clove fresh garlic
- 2 tablespoons white wine vinegar
- 1 tablespoon sherry wine vinegar
- 8 cherry tomatoes, halved
- 8 scallions, finely chopped
- Freshly ground black pepper, to taste

Calabacitas Salad

Summer squash of any kind is great in this fresh salad, but I prefer a combination of baby zucchini and small yellow crookneck squash. The piñon nuts make this very New Mexican, as piñon trees abound in the nearby mountains.

Combine basil, garlic, pequín, oil, and vinegar in a blender or food processor. Process until very well blended. Place zucchini, crookneck squash, and tomatoes in a brightly-colored salad bowl. Toss together with dressing and sprinkle with piñon nuts. Refrigerate about 1 hour before serving and serve chilled. Makes 4 servings

- ⅓ cup fresh basil leaves
- 2 cloves garlic
- ¼ teaspoon pequín quebrado, or to taste
- ½ cup extra virgin olive oil
- 3 tablespoons balsamic vinegar, or to taste
- 2 small zucchini, thinly sliced
- 2 small yellow crookneck squash, thinly sliced
- 1 pint cherry tomatoes, halved
- ⅓ cup piñon nuts

Grilled Tuna Salad

1 pound fresh tuna steak, cut 1-inch thick

⅓ cup extra virgin olive oil

2 cups quartered cherry tomatoes

1 cup pickled Tuscan peppers

1 medium-hot red onion, thinly sliced and separated into rings

2 sprigs fresh thyme

2 cloves garlic, minced

2 tablespoons red wine vinegar

1 tablespoon hot prepared mustard

2 teaspoons mustard seeds

2 teaspoons Worcestershire sauce

Salt, to taste

Freshly ground black pepper, to taste

1 head romaine lettuce

What could be more soothing than seafood and salad? The combination somehow makes summer seem cooler—even when you include a spirited helping of Tuscan peppers. Crisp garlic toast makes a nice accompaniment for this salad.

Prepare a bed of hot coals or heat a heavy skillet over high heat until very hot. Brush tuna on both sides with some of the oil. Brush barbecue grill or griddle with oil. Cook tuna for 2 to 3 minutes on each side, or until browned on outside but still very rare in center. Cool tuna briefly, and then cut in 1-inch squares. In a medium bowl, combine tuna squares, tomatoes, peppers, onion, and thyme. Set aside.

In a separate bowl, combine garlic, remaining oil, vinegar, mustard, mustard seeds, and Worcestershire sauce. Whisk to blend, taste, and season with salt and pepper. To serve, line a platter or 4 individual plates with lettuce. Fold garlic dressing into tuna mixture, and then arrange salad on platter or individual plates. ⊰ Makes 4 servings

Rio Party Salad

2 (1-pound) cans hearts of palm, drained

1 pint cherry tomatoes, halved

⅔ cup extra virgin olive oil

¼ cup sherry wine vinegar

1 clove garlic, finely minced

½ teaspoon salt, or to taste

1 teaspoon caribe (crushed Northern New Mexico red chile)

1 head Boston lettuce

1 head red leaf lettuce

This light salad is simple to prepare and lovely to look at with a flavor that enhances any spicy-hot entrée. I'm especially fond of serving this salad at buffets as an accompaniment to a few different casseroles. It makes for a cozy, lingering evening; guests can eat as often and as much as they wish, and the hostess can relax, since nothing wilts or gets cold (just keep the hot dishes warm on a warming tray).

Place hearts of palm and tomatoes in a medium bowl. Combine oil, vinegar, garlic, salt, and caribe. Pour over tomato mixture and stir gently to coat evenly. Let stand at room temperature throughout the day, stirring often and spooning dressing over vegetables. About 2 hours before serving, cover and refrigerate.

To serve, arrange Boston and red leaf lettuce leaves around edge of a large platter. Carefully place hearts of palm spoke-fashion around the edge, and place tomatoes in the center. Drizzle all with dressing and serve.
⊰ Makes 10 servings

Hot Spinach Salad with Smoked Salmon

This light yet succulent salad is a great choice when you want to serve something different for brunch, lunch, or a late-night treat.

Rinse spinach very well. Discard stems and any tough or wilted leaves. Heat 2 tablespoons of the oil in a large, heavy skillet or wok. When oil is hot, add spinach, ginger, and caribe. Cook over medium-high heat, stirring, just until spinach is wilted but not fully cooked. Set aside.

In a small saucepan, combine remaining oil, vinegar, sugar, mustard, salt, and cream or evaporated milk. Heat until almost simmering. Remove from heat and stir in dill. Divide hot spinach among 6 plates, and top with smoked salmon slices. Divide mustard dressing evenly, drizzling it uniformly over each salad. Garnish with onion rings and serve. ⊰ Makes 6 servings

2 pounds fresh spinach
¾ cup extra virgin olive oil
1 teaspoon chopped fresh ginger, or to taste
1 tablespoon caribe (crushed Northern New Mexico red chile)
⅓ cup raspberry or red wine vinegar
1 tablespoon sugar
3 tablespoons Dijon-style mustard
¾ teaspoon salt, or to taste
½ cup whipping cream or evaporated skim milk
⅓ cup chopped fresh dill
½ pound smoked salmon, very thinly sliced
6 very thin slices red onion, separated into rings

Red Hot Warm Potato Salad

This salad is a great way to celebrate the arrival of spring's delicately pink baby potatoes. We first made this in the country and enjoyed it outside on the patio with Hotter Than Hell Buffet Barbecued Chicken (see page 81).

Scrub potatoes and cut in halves or quarters, depending on size. Cook in boiling water about 20 minutes, or until tender. Meanwhile, hard-cook eggs 15 minutes, and then drain (see Note). When potatoes are done, drain well and immediately add butter to saucepan with potatoes. Cover and set aside until butter is melted, and then stir until butter is thoroughly combined with potatoes. Add parsley, jalapeños, jalapeño juice, green onions, and radishes. Shell and chop hard-cooked eggs, and then fold in. Stir in mustard, mayonnaise, salt, and pepper. Taste and adjust seasonings. Serve at once.
⊰ Makes 4 servings

8 small red, thin-skinned potatoes
3 eggs
¼ cup unsalted butter
2 tablespoons minced fresh parsley or 1 tablespoon dried parsley flakes
1 tablespoon finely minced pickled or fresh jalapeño chiles
1 tablespoon juice from pickled jalapeño chiles, or to taste
2 green onions, thinly sliced
4 red radishes, thinly sliced
1 teaspoon prepared mustard
¼ cup mayonnaise
Salt, to taste
Freshly ground black pepper, to taste

Note: To get perfect results when hard-cooking eggs, start them in cold water to cover, with 2 tablespoons vinegar, preferably white, and 1 tablespoon salt. Bring to a simmer, cover, and cook for 15 minutes. Remove from water and place in cold water. These will easily peel and not have a sulphur ring.

Thai Hot Beef Salad

1 small head romaine lettuce

1 small head red leaf lettuce

1 head Belgian endive

¾ cup peanut oil

¼ cup fresh lime juice

3 tablespoons dark soy sauce

1 pound beef sirloin, cut in 3-inch-long and ¼-inch-wide strips

1 (1-inch) piece fresh ginger, peeled and finely grated

1 tablespoon packed dark brown sugar

2 large cloves garlic, minced

2 or 3 fresh jalapeño chiles, finely minced

½ cup coarsely chopped fresh cilantro

3 red-ripe tomatoes, cut in wedges

2 green onions, finely chopped

4 green onions, butterflied (see Note)

Note: To butterfly a green onion, leave the onion whole and shred the green tops lengthwise with a sharp knife for ⅔ of their length.

The Thai are masters in achieving subtle flavor combinations, even with the hottest chiles and spices. Whenever I'm in Thailand, I can never get enough of their hot, spicy dishes. This one is an unusual entrée salad.

Tear romaine and leaf lettuce leaves into bite-size pieces. Carefully remove whole endive leaves from stalk. Enclose greens in plastic bags and refrigerate.

In a shallow dish, combine 2 tablespoons each of the oil, lime juice, and soy sauce. Add beef strips to this marinade, stir well, and let stand at least 1 hour at room temperature.

To make the dressing, combine ½ cup of the oil, the remaining 2 tablespoons lime juice, remaining 1 tablespoon soy sauce, ginger, brown sugar, garlic, and jalapeños in a blender or food processor. Process until puréed. Set aside.

In a heavy skillet, heat remaining 2 tablespoons of the oil. When oil is hot, drain beef strips, reserving the marinade. Add beef to skillet and quickly stir-fry just until browned on the outside. Mix reserved marinade into dressing.

To serve, place chilled greens in a large heatproof salad bowl. Top with hot beef strips. Rinse out hot skillet with dressing, scraping down sides and bottom to get any remaining browned bits. Pour dressing over beef, and then add cilantro, tomatoes, and chopped green onions. Toss well to coat. Garnish with butterflied green onions and serve immediately. ⚔ Makes 4 servings

Tropical Fruit Salad

½ cantaloupe, cut in 1-inch cubes

½ honeydew melon, cut in 1-inch cubes

1 mango, peeled and sliced

2 cups cubed watermelon

⅓ cup honey

⅓ cup fresh lime juice

¼ cup minced fresh mint leaves

1 small, perfect head Boston or Romaine lettuce

Tinged with fresh mint and a honeyed lime dressing, this salad is a great accompaniment to any hot, spicy dish. If fresh mint leaves are unavailable, substitute a good-quality mint jelly and decrease the amount of honey by about 2 tablespoons.

Combine cantaloupe, honeydew, mango, and watermelon. In a blender, process honey, lime juice, and mint until well blended. Drizzle over fruit. Line a clear glass bowl or any pretty salad bowl with lettuce leaves and spoon in fruit mixture. Serve slightly chilled. ⚔ Makes 4 to 6 servings

Holiday Salad of Peppers and Endive

This salad is unbelievably pretty, with pale, pale green endive and scarlet bell peppers cut in ever-so-skinny slivers. The salsa can be made hours or even days in advance.

To prepare Salsa Vinaigrette, combine all salsa ingredients in a jar. Stir or shake until well mixed, and let stand at least 30 minutes at room temperature. To serve salad, toss endive and bell peppers with vinaigrette. Line a salad bowl with lettuce leaves and top with dressed endive and peppers.

➤ Makes 6 servings

Note: If Belgian endive is not available, you may substitute 3 cups green bell pepper strips, jicama strips, or sliced fresh mushrooms.

3 small heads Belgian endive, cut lengthwise in ¼-inch-wide strips (see Note)

2 large red bell peppers, cut in ¼-inch-wide strips

1 small head Boston lettuce

SALSA VINAIGRETTE

¼ cup red wine vinegar

1 clove garlic, minced

2 tablespoons minced onion

1 fresh mild green chile, parched (see page 6), peeled, seeded, and minced

1 small tomato, finely chopped

½ cup extra virgin olive oil

Acapulco Salad

Seafood of the Mexican waters, a palette of fresh, colorful vegetables, and a Mexican-inspired dressing add up to a delightful salad—a perfect choice for a light entrée. It's best to use Spanish olive oil in the dressing, but if you can't find it, substitute any other good-quality olive oil.

In a large saucepan, combine beer, water, bay leaves, peppercorns, and salt. Bring to a boil. Add fish, cover, and turn off heat. Allow to cool, covered, about 15 minutes, or until fish is opaque throughout. (Fish cooks as liquid cools; this extra-gentle method of cooking keeps the flesh intact.)

Meanwhile, cook fresh corn in boiling water until tender. Drain, and then cut kernels from cobs. Combine corn, tomatoes, yellow bell pepper or wax pepper, poblano chile or green pepper, jalapeño or serrano, and green onion. Set aside.

To prepare dressing, whisk together salsa or tomatillos, lime juice, and oil. Taste and adjust heat. If not hot enough (or if you used tomatillos), add jalapeño juice to taste. Toss dressing with vegetables and place mixture in a large salad bowl. Drain fish. Gently flake and scatter around edge of bowl. Sprinkle with cilantro, if desired.

➤ Makes 4 servings

1 cup beer

2 cups water

2 bay leaves

12 whole black peppercorns

½ teaspoon salt

1 pound red snapper fillets

3 ears fresh corn

1 large or 2 medium red-ripe tomatoes, cut in thin wedges

½ yellow bell pepper or ½ sweet yellow wax pepper, cut in thin strips

½ fresh poblano chile or green bell pepper, cut in thin strips

1 or more small fresh hot jalapeño or serrano chiles, finely minced

3 green onions (including some of the green tops), thinly sliced

¼ cup hot green salsa or chopped canned tomatillos

2 tablespoon fresh lime juice

¼ cup extra virgin Spanish olive oil

Juice from pickled jalapeño chiles

2 tablespoons minced fresh cilantro, if desired

Watercress-Mushroom Salad, Santa Fe-Style

½ cup extra virgin olive oil or walnut oil

2 large cloves garlic, finely minced

1 teaspoon minced fresh rosemary or ½ teaspoon dried rosemary

1 teaspoon minced fresh tarragon or ½ teaspoon dried tarragon

1 teaspoon minced fresh thyme or ½ teaspoon dried thyme

2 teaspoons minced fresh basil or 1 teaspoon dried basil

1 tablespoon Dijon-style mustard

1 medium bunch watercress, rinsed well and stemmed

1 large head Belgian endive, leaves removed from stalk

2 cups fresh white button or brown-skinned French mushrooms, very thinly sliced

1 teaspoon caribe (crushed Northern New Mexico red chile)

2 ½ tablespoons fresh lime juice

I developed this favorite salad dressing to go over my very favorite combination of salad ingredients—watercress, Belgian endive, and mushrooms. Since all of us prefer this dressing over any other, I make tons of the base and keep it constantly in our refrigerator. When I want to use it, I just remove the jar from the fridge and run it briefly under hot water to warm the oil. (For space reasons, I add only about half the oil to the herb-mustard mixture, and then add fresh oil when combining the salad ingredients.)

The Santa Fe part of this salad is the watercress—we always used our own fresh, peppery, spring-grown sprigs—and the dash of crushed Northern New Mexico caribe chiles.

Combine oil, garlic, herbs, and mustard, and let stand at least 30 minutes at room temperature while you prepare the salad ingredients. Arrange watercress, endive, and mushrooms in a wooden or glass bowl. Refrigerate until cold. To serve, sprinkle with caribe, add dressing, and lace with lime juice. Toss and serve. ⌁ Makes 4 servings

Grilled Mexican Vegetable Salad

2 large ears of corn, husked

1 large red bell pepper

4 tomatillos, husked and halved

2 medium tomatoes

1 jalapeño chile

2 to 3 (½-inch) slices jicama, peeled

5 tablespoons extra virgin olive oil

½ cup peeled, diced carrots

⅓ cup thinly sliced green onions

½ cup chopped fresh cilantro

3 tablespoons fresh lime juice

2 ½ teaspoons grated lime peel

¼ teaspoon ground cumin

Salt, to taste

Freshly ground black pepper, to taste

This salad can double as a salsa and is wonderful over grilled fish or chicken. Plan to make it at least an hour or even a day ahead. If chilling overnight, be sure to warm up to room temperature for at least an hour before serving.

Heat a grill, stovetop, or electric grill to medium. Brush corn, bell pepper, tomatillos, tomatoes, jalapeño, and jicama lightly with 1 tablespoon of the olive oil. Grill each vegetable until tender and brown in spots, turning occasionally, about 10 minutes. Cool slightly. Cut off corn kernels, and place in large bowl. Dice and chop remaining grilled vegetables. Add carrots, green onions, and cilantro and toss.

In a small bowl, whisk lime juice, lime peel, cumin, and remaining 4 tablespoons oil. Mix lime dressing into salad and coat well. Season to taste with salt and pepper. ⌁ Makes 8 servings

Shrimp and Mesclun Salad with
Spicy Crisp Pecans, Mango, and Gorgonzola

Shrimp and Mesclun Salad with Spicy Crisp Pecans, Mango, and Gorgonzola

¼ cup pecans, toasted

½ cup extra virgin olive or walnut oil

2 teaspoons Barbecue Rub (see page 125)

32 colossal shrimp

1 teaspoon shrimp and crab boil

¼ cup balsamic vinegar

1 clove fresh garlic, minced

1 tablespoon Dijon mustard

Salt, to taste

Freshly ground black pepper, to taste

1 (12-ounce) bag mesclun greens

1 large or 2 small mangos, peeled and diced

½ cup crumbled Gorgonzola or bleu cheese

This salad is very versatile, and it works with almost any kind of seafood. Or, you can just serve the salad without any seafood for a lighter option.

Preheat oven to 350°F. In a small bowl, toss the pecans with 1 tablespoon of the oil and the barbecue rub. Spread pecans on a baking sheet and toast for 10 to 15 minutes, watching carefully to prevent over-browning. Set aside.

In a large pot, add shrimp, 2 cups water, and shrimp and crab boil. Cook shrimp until done. Drain and cool.

To prepare the dressing, combine remaining oil, balsamic vinegar, garlic, mustard, salt, and pepper. Whisk well. Taste and adjust seasonings as desired.

To assemble the salads, drain and rinse the greens. Place a mound of greens on each of 4 plates. Using 8 shrimp per plate, alternate shrimp and mango slices in a radial design around the plate's edge. Garnish with toasted pecans and cheese, and drizzle with dressing. ⤳ Makes 4 servings

Peppy Pasta Salad

1 pound dried mostaccioli, twists, or other substantial pasta

1 cup mayonnaise

½ teaspoon pequín quebrado, or to taste

3 large or 6 small cloves garlic, chopped

1 ½ tablespoons fresh lime juice, or to taste

2 teaspoons Dijon-style or hot German mustard

2 cups well-rinsed, stemmed, lightly packed fresh spinach leaves, cut in narrow ribbons

1 fresh or pickled jalapeño chile, finely slivered

1 red bell pepper, cut in long, thin strips

6 pickled red cherry peppers, halved

1 cup fresh snow peas, cut in diagonal slivers

1 cup marinated artichoke hearts, drained

You can vary this salad in dozens of ways. The following combination is a favorite of mine, but you may wish to substitute any seasonal vegetables for the artichoke hearts, peas, spinach, and peppers.

Following package directions, cook pasta in boiling water just until tender. Drain and set aside. Combine mayonnaise, pequín, garlic, lime juice, and mustard in a food processor, and process until smooth.

In a medium bowl, combine pasta, spinach, jalapeño, bell pepper, cherry peppers, snow peas, and artichokes. Add dressing and toss lightly. Taste and adjust seasonings. Before serving, refrigerate until cool, at least 2 hours or as long as overnight. ⤳ Makes 6 servings

Light Meals

Playing with Fire

SATISFYING MEALS don't have to be multi-course feasts! The recipes in this chapter are meals in themselves, requiring only your favorite beverage and perhaps a crisp salad as accompaniments. The secret is flavor—and lots of it. Hot seasonings such as chiles, pepper, mustard, ginger, and horseradish really help appease the heartiest appetites, even if the serving sizes are modest.

These light meals are versatile and varied. Serve Hot French Eggs for breakfast, Jon's Veggie Crepe Cake for brunch, Nacho-Sauced Cartwheels for dinner, and Beautiful Bagel Sandwiches for a late-night snack. Many of the recipes are quick to whip up, too, so keep them in mind for days when you're short on time.

Spanish Tortilla, Ensenada-Style

1 cup extra virgin Spanish olive oil (see Note)

4 medium potatoes, peeled and finely diced or grated

1 medium onion, finely chopped

8 eggs

1 teaspoon pequín quebrado, or to taste

1 teaspoon salt

Ranchero Sauce (see page 129), if desired

Note: With a nonstick pan and nonstick cooking spray, you can decrease the oil to ½ cup or less. However, you do need enough oil to brown the potatoes and to cook the egg mixture so that it lightly browns without sticking.

A Mexican tortilla is flat, unleavened bread—but it is not so with this Spanish tortilla! It's a delicious potato omelet spiced Mexican-style with pequín chiles. This Castilian delight should always be cooked in the best olive oil you can find, preferably extra virgin Spanish olive oil.

Heat ¼ cup of the oil to smoking in each of 2 heavy skillets (at least 12 inches in diameter). Add half the potatoes to each pan and cook, stirring often, until golden and crisp. Add half the onion to each skillet and continue to cook, stirring often, until potatoes are well browned and tender but have no blackened edges. Remove from heat and cool for about 5 minutes.

Meanwhile, in each of 2 bowls, beat together 4 eggs, ½ teaspoon pequín, and ½ teaspoon salt. Add 1 pan of cooked potato-onion mixture to each bowl of eggs, and stir well. Add ¼ cup more oil to each skillet and heat until smoking. Then add 1 bowl of egg mixture to each skillet. Cook, shaking skillet often, until bottom of omelet is slightly golden. Lift edges often with a spatula to check, running spatula around edge of omelet to free it. When omelets are almost firm, turn them. (Place a plate the same size as skillet over each skillet, and invert omelet onto plate. Then slip omelet back into skillet, browned side up.) Cook, shaking skillet, until second side is golden, and then slide out of pan and serve at once. These omelets are generally served cut in quarters—serve 1 quarter as a light course of a meal, 2 quarters as a breakfast, lunch, or brunch main dish. If desired, serve omelets with Ranchero Sauce on the side.

⤙ Makes 4 to 8 servings

Zucchini Julienne Tossed with Pesto

Julienned zucchini is a light substitute for pasta—and a very flavorful one, especially when sauced with this spicy, chile-flavored pesto. You'll only need about half the pesto for this much zucchini. I've deliberately given you a large-quantity pesto recipe, since the sauce keeps for several months in the freezer or refrigerator. (If you don't want any leftover, just cut the pesto recipe in half.)

In a food processor, combine garlic, basil leaves, piñon nuts, chiles, and oil. Process just until puréed; do not overprocess. Pour mixture into a 3-quart bowl and add ¾ cup Parmesan cheese, ⅓ cup Romano cheese, and butter. Mix with a spoon, sprinkling in very hot tap water a little at a time until mixture has the consistency of whipping cream. Set pesto aside.

Using a food processor, julienne zucchini lengthwise into matchstick-size strips. Into a steamer or large saucepan, pour water to a depth of about 2 inches and bring to a boil. Scatter zucchini strips in steamer basket and set basket in pan; basket should not touch water. Cover pan and steam zucchini about 2 minutes, or until strands droop slightly when lifted. Immediately transfer zucchini to a warmed serving dish. Spoon a generous amount of pesto onto zucchini. Using 2 wooden spoons to keep the tender strands from breaking, lightly toss zucchini with sauce. Serve immediately with additional cheese on top, if desired.

⌇ Makes about 6 light servings

2 large cloves garlic

3 cups slightly packed fresh basil leaves

⅓ cup piñon nuts

¾ cup parched (see page 6), peeled, seeded fresh New Mexico hot green chiles

¾ cup extra virgin olive oil

¾ cup freshly grated Parmesan cheese

⅓ cup freshly grated Romano cheese

⅓ cup unsalted butter, room temperature (see Note)

2 large or 3 medium zucchini, ends trimmed

Additional freshly grated Parmesan or Romano cheese

Note: For less fat, omit the butter.

Fish Tacos

2 tablespoons fresh lime juice

¼ cup oil

1 tablespoon pickled jalapeño juice

¼ teaspoon salt

⅛ teaspoon crushed black pepper

1 pound haddock, cod, red snapper, salmon, or any firm-fleshed white fish

12 (6-inch) soft white corn tortillas, warmed

Hotter Than Hell Salsa (see page 126)

Note: These tacos are a great light snack as is, or they may be topped with a crisp, fresh coleslaw: combine 6 tablespoons olive oil, 2 tablespoons cider vinegar, and 3 cups thinly slivered red or green cabbage and toss well.

Fish is the perfect filling for tacos, and I like most any kind of fish or seafood. Grilling the fish or seafood is so much lighter than the batter-fried variety often found. Serve these tacos already filled and folded or in a taco bar, where each guest places their own fish and salsa in the warm tortilla. The crunch of the optional coleslaw is highly recommended.

In a medium bowl, combine lime juice, oil, jalapeño juice, salt, and pepper. Marinate fish for approximately 10 minutes.

Meanwhile, heat grill or broiler to hottest setting. Remove fish from marinade and gently shake to remove excess. In a well-ventilated kitchen (the oil in the marinade will smoke, making it necessary to use a vent) or outdoors, grill fish until opaque and flaky, about 2 to 3 minutes per side. While fish is cooking, heat the tortillas in a plastic bag in the microwave for 1 minute. Keep warm in a tortilla warmer or towel. Break fish into bite-sized pieces, and place in folded corn tortillas. Top with salsa, and, if desired, coleslaw (see Note).

⤛ Makes 4 to 6 servings

Chili Combo

1 tablespoon unsalted butter, room temperature

3 cups chili

1 cup tortilla chips

TOPPING

2 cups milk

1 tablespoon unsalted butter

3 eggs, separated

¼ cup all-purpose flour

¼ teaspoon salt

¾ cup grated Monterey Jack cheese

4 teaspoons ground pure New Mexico hot red chile

⅔ cup creamed corn

A fluffy soufflé topping mellows the bite of hot chile in this simple, yet elegant-looking dish. It's a great way to use up leftover tortilla chips and chili.

Preheat oven to 350°F. Butter a 9-inch-square baking pan and set aside. To prepare topping, scald 1 ½ cups of the milk with butter in a saucepan. Cool. In another saucepan, beat egg yolks until blended. Beat in remaining ½ cup milk, flour, and salt. Cook over low heat, stirring until thickened. Remove from heat. Slowly add cooled scalded milk, whisking well. Gently stir in cheese, ground chile, and corn. Beat egg whites until they hold stiff peaks, and fold in to milk and cheese mixture. Set topping aside.

In buttered baking pan, layer chili and tortilla chips, ending with a layer of chili. Cover evenly with topping. Bake, uncovered, for 45 minutes, or until a wooden pick inserted in center of topping comes out clean.

⤛ Makes about 6 servings

Tasty Tomato Taglierini

A totally sunny experience! The blissful flavor of sun-dried tomatoes is even more tempting when spiced.

Lift tomatoes from cup, and cut in ⅛-inch-wide slivers. In a serving bowl, whisk together eggs, slivered tomatoes and their oil, cheeses, parsley, caribe or crushed red pepper, garlic, and lemon juice until blended.

   Following package directions, cook taglierini in boiling water just until tender to bite; drain well. Add drained pasta to egg mixture, and lift with 2 forks to mix. Season with salt, if desired, and pepper. Serve immediately.

   ⌁ Makes 2 to 4 servings

1 cup sun-dried tomatoes in oil
2 eggs
¼ cup mixed freshly grated Romano and
   Parmesan cheeses
2 tablespoons chopped fresh parsley
1 tablespoon caribe (crushed Northern
   New Mexico red chile) or Italian
   crushed hot red pepper
2 cloves garlic, minced
1 tablespoon fresh lemon juice
8 ounces dried taglierini
Salt, if desired
Freshly ground black pepper, to taste

Nacho-Sauced Cartwheels

Cheery pasta cartwheels in a creamy, vegetable-laden sauce make a delightful dish. Though Italian-inspired, it's not Italian all the way—nacho-sliced pickled jalapeño chiles add a snappy Mexican accent.

Thoroughly rinse leeks, and then thinly slice leeks crosswise. Melt butter in a large skillet, add leeks, and cook over medium heat about 10 minutes, stirring several times.

   Meanwhile, thinly slice zucchini. Thinly slice mushrooms lengthwise so all will have some stem attached to cap, if possible. Chop tomatoes. Add zucchini, mushrooms, tomatoes, and basil to leeks and stir-fry over medium-high heat until zucchini is barely tender; it should remain bright green. Stir in 1 cup cream, jalapeños, ¼ cup each of the Parmesan and Roman cheeses, nutmeg, and pepper. Taste and adjust seasonings. Just before mixture comes to a boil, turn off heat.

   Following package directions, cook pasta in boiling water just until tender to bite. When pasta is just tender, drain well and return to cooking pot. Pour sauce over pasta and stir well. Heat briefly over high heat, stirring constantly. If pasta has absorbed too much sauce, gently stir in ½ cup more cream. Combine remaining ¼ cup each Parmesan and Romano cheeses and pass at the table. Serve immediately.

   ⌁ Makes 4 to 6 servings

2 medium leeks
¼ cup unsalted butter
1 medium zucchini
½ pound fresh mushrooms
6 to 8 cherry tomatoes
1 tablespoon chopped fresh basil or 1
   teaspoon dried basil
1 to 1 ½ cups light cream
½ cup nacho-sliced pickled jalapeño
   chiles, or to taste
½ cup freshly grated Parmesan cheese
½ cup freshly grated Romano cheese
Freshly grated nutmeg, to taste
Freshly ground black pepper, to taste
1 pound dried cartwheel-shaped pasta

Tasty Tomato Taglierini

Sombrero Jalapa

Eggs to put your hat on and get you going! That's one way to translate Sombrero Jalapa, the southwestern version of eggs Benedict. This dish is superb for brunch; make it with leftover or freshly made Chile con Queso.

Preheat oven to lowest heat, and warm 4 plates. Heat Chile con Queso just until warm. Poach eggs, and set aside. Heat oil in a heavy skillet. Soft-fry tortillas, 1 at a time, in oil. Remove tortillas to a plate, and lightly pat down with a paper towel to remove excess oil.

   To assemble Jalapas, place a tortilla on each plate. Top each with 2 eggs, and then with ¼ cup of the Chile con Queso. Sprinkle servings evenly with caribe, and garnish with lettuce and tomatoes. ⊰ Makes 4 servings

1 cup Chile con Queso (see page 14)
8 eggs
¼ cup vegetable oil (see Note)
4 (6-inch) corn tortillas
1 tablespoon caribe (crushed Northern New Mexico red chile)
1 cup or more shredded Romaine or iceberg lettuce
4 cherry tomatoes, cut in "roses"

Note: For a lower-calorie version, heat the tortillas, 1 at a time, over a gas or electric burner until just hot and barely crisped instead of frying in oil.

Pristine Penne

This zippy, mushroom-laced red sauce dresses sharp-ended penne pasta beautifully.

Heat oil in a large, deep pot. Add mushrooms and cook until mushrooms are lightly browned and all liquid has evaporated. Add garlic, tomatoes, onion, salt, herbs, and 2 teaspoons crushed red pepper. Bring to a boil, reduce heat, cover, and simmer about 1 hour or until flavors are blended. Taste and adjust seasonings.

   Following package directions, cook pasta in boiling water just until tender to bite. Drain pasta well and toss with sauce. Serve with cheeses on the side and additional crushed red pepper, if desired. ⊰ Makes 4 servings

¼ cup olive oil
1 pound fresh mushrooms, thinly sliced
2 cloves garlic, minced
1 (32-ounce) can Italian plum tomatoes, mashed with a fork
½ cup finely chopped onion
½ teaspoon salt, or to taste
2 tablespoons chopped fresh oregano or 1 tablespoon dried oregano
1 teaspoon chopped fresh rosemary or ½ teaspoon dried rosemary
1 tablespoon chopped fresh marjoram or 1 tablespoon dried basil
2 teaspoons Italian crushed hot red pepper, or to taste
12 ounces dried penne pasta
4 ounces grated Romano cheese
4 ounces grated Parmesan cheese
Additional Italian crushed hot red pepper, if desired

Hot French Eggs

¼ cup unsalted butter

½ cup coarsely chopped chicken livers

½ cup chopped shallots or green onions

¾ cup sliced fresh mushrooms

¼ cup all-purpose flour

¾ cup double-strength beef broth

Salt, to taste

½ teaspoon freshly ground white pepper, or to taste

½ cup dry red wine

About 1 tablespoon unsalted butter, room temperature

8 eggs

Chopped fresh chives or parsley

These rich-tasting eggs are right from a village in France! The spice is American, though. Serve as a brunch, light lunch, or supper entrée with a nice bottle of red wine, warm, crusty French bread, and perhaps a salad.

Melt ¼ cup butter in a medium, heavy skillet, and then add chicken livers. Cook until livers start to brown. Add shallots or green onions and mushrooms and cook until browned. Reduce heat and sprinkle flour over livers and vegetables, stirring constantly. When flour starts to brown, stir in broth, salt, white pepper, and wine. Simmer, uncovered, stirring often, for 15 to 20 minutes.

Preheat oven to 350°F. Butter 4 small French cassoulet dishes or ovenproof bowls. Place 2 tablespoons of the chicken liver sauce in each (keep remaining sauce warm), and then carefully break 2 eggs on top of each dish. Bake, uncovered, for 15 to 20 minutes, or until eggs are firm. When eggs are done, top each dish equally with remaining liver sauce, and sprinkle with chives or parsley.

Makes 4 servings

Southern California Omelet

2 tablespoons unsalted butter

1 (10- to 12-inch) flour tortilla

2 green onions, finely minced

½ Hass avocado, pitted, peeled, and cut in ½-inch cubes

½ medium tomato, cut in ¼-inch cubes

3 eggs

1 tablespoon tequila or water

¼ cup Margarita Jalapeño Salsa (see page 128)

¼ cup dairy sour cream

2 tablespoons chopped fresh cilantro

This omelet is especially popular just north of the California-Mexico border, yet it's very easy to make and enjoy anywhere! Serve it for a nice light meal or snack.

Melt butter in a large skillet or on a griddle. Place tortilla in skillet and lightly cook both sides; do not crisp. Set aside on a serving plate. Add green onion, avocado, and tomato to skillet. Stir 1 to 2 minutes, or until heated through. Beat together eggs and tequila or water, and pour over vegetables in skillet. Cook until set on bottom. Carefully turn over as directed for Spanish Tortilla, Ensenada-Style on page 43, and cook on other side until as done as desired. (Or cook without turning: as edges set, constantly lift them with a spatula and allow uncooked egg to flow underneath. Cook until omelet is as firm as desired.) Slide omelet out of pan on top of tortilla. Top with salsa, spoon sour cream in center, and garnish with cilantro. Makes 1 serving

Chile-Crusted Chorizo Quiche

Quiche is usually quite mild in flavor—but never say no to this sassy version. It's good for brunch, lunch, or supper, and it's easy to put together, especially if you already have parched green chiles on hand in the freezer. If you'd like to turn down the heat a bit, just substitute fried tortillas for the green-chile crust (see Pastel de Pescado on page 72 for instructions on making the tortilla crust).

Preheat oven to 375°F. Butter a 9-inch pie plate, preferably ovenproof glass or pottery. Line pie plate with chiles, opening each one out completely and arranging with points at center of plate. Arrange chorizo in an even layer across bottom of chile crust.

In a separate bowl, beat together eggs, cilantro, and cream. Very carefully pour into pie plate, being sure not to disturb distribution of sausage. Evenly sprinkle cheese over egg mixture, and then place onion rings in a circle just inside edge of pie plate. Sprinkle caribe or pequín evenly over all and bake for 30 minutes, or until a knife inserted in the center comes out clean. Serve with salsa on the side, if desired.

☙ Makes 6 servings

1 tablespoon unsalted butter, room temperature

6 to 8 large fresh New Mexico hot green chiles, parched (see page 6), peeled, seeded, and de-ribbed

½ pound chorizo or hot Italian sausage, casings removed, meat crumbled, browned, and drained (see Tip)

4 eggs

1 tablespoon chopped fresh cilantro

1 cup light cream

1 cup grated Monterey Jack cheese (see Tip)

1 small onion, thinly sliced and separated into rings

1 tablespoon caribe (crushed Northern New Mexico red chile) or 1 teaspoon pequín quebrado, or to taste

½ cup hot salsa, if desired

Tip: To vary the filling, substitute almost any kind of meat, crab, shrimp, fish, or chicken for the sausage, and use Cheddar in place of the Jack.

Quick Tricks

Make these quick, Mexican-influenced open-face sandwiches when short on time.

Preheat broiler. Place a slice of Cheddar on each piece of bread, and then place bread in a broiler pan. Top each sandwich with 2 bacon slices, and then top evenly with salsa and green onions. Cut remaining cheeses in ½-inch-wide strips. Place Swiss strips diagonally across each sandwich, leaving a space between strips. Crisscross jack strips at right angles over Swiss strips. Sprinkle caribe and peppers or chiles over sandwiches. Broil until cheeses are melted; serve hot.

☙ Makes 4 servings

8 slices Cheddar cheese

8 slices whole-grain whole-wheat bread, toasted

16 slices bacon, crisply cooked and drained

¼ cup Margarita Jalapeño Salsa (see page 128) or other hot salsa

4 green onions, thinly sliced

8 slices Swiss cheese

4 slices Monterey Jack cheese

2 tablespoons caribe (crushed Northern New Mexico red chile)

4 pickled Tuscan peppers or jalapeño chiles, thinly sliced

Chile-Crusted Chorizo Quiche

Beautiful Bagel Sandwiches

Lavishly layered open-face sandwiches, featuring some unexpected but entirely delicious flavor combinations, make a satisfying lunch or snack.

To prepare Horseradish Sauce, mix all ingredients. Spread a layer of sauce on each bagel half. Sprinkle sprouts on each half, and then layer with cheese and salmon. Top each half with kiwifruit slices arranged in an overlapping ring. (If desired, heat the sandwiches to melt cheese before adding kiwifruit.) ⌁ Makes 4 to 8 servings

4 bagels, sliced in half
1 cup alfalfa sprouts
4 ounces Monterey Jack cheese, sliced
6 ounces smoked salmon, thinly sliced
2 kiwifruit, peeled and thinly sliced

HORSERADISH SAUCE
¼ cup dairy sour cream
¼ cup mayonnaise
¼ cup freshly grated horseradish

Touchdown Chile Puff

This make-ahead dish is terrific for brunch on Super Bowl Sunday—or for brunch, lunch, or supper on any other day of the week. It's great plain, but you may want to add chorizo, ham, or a favorite breakfast meat. Cornbread or hot flour tortillas plus perhaps a salad or some fresh fruit nicely complement the puff.

Preheat oven to 325°F. Butter a 9 x 13-inch baking dish or other 3 quart casserole dish. Combine cheeses, chiles, and 2 tablespoons of the flour. Mix well, and then distribute evenly in buttered casserole dish.

Beat egg yolks well with a whisk or an electric mixer. Beat in remaining 6 tablespoons flour, cream, salt, oregano, and cumin. Then beat egg whites with baking powder until they hold stiff, moist peaks. Fold whites into egg yolk mixture. Spoon over cheese mixture in casserole. (At this point, you may cover and refrigerate 1 to 2 hours.) Bake, uncovered, about 1 hour, or until top is golden brown and a knife inserted in center comes out clean. Cool about 10 minutes before cutting and serving. ⌁ Makes 10 to 12 servings

1 tablespoon unsalted butter, room temperature
1 pound coarsely grated Monterey Jack cheese
1 pound coarsely grated sharp Cheddar cheese
1 (7-ounce) can diced green chiles
½ cup all-purpose flour
6 eggs, separated
⅔ cup light cream
½ teaspoon salt
½ teaspoon ground oregano, preferably Mexican
¼ teaspoon ground cumin
¼ teaspoon baking powder

Beautiful Bagel Sandwiches

Italian Omelet Roll

This impressive rolled omelet offers a kaleidoscope of colors and flavors: hot sausage, pickled peppers, and fiery pequín tempered with mild mozzarella cheese and the delicate omelet base. Not as difficult to make as it looks, the omelet is quick to put together. Once baked and assembled, it must be served immediately.

Butter a 10 x 15-inch jelly-roll pan. Cover bottom of pan with a piece of waxed paper, cut to size. Butter paper.

Preheat oven to 350°F. Beat egg whites until stiff, and set aside. Combine salt, pequín, and egg yolks, and beat with a whisk until blended. Fold whites and yolks together. Turn egg mixture into prepared pan, carefully smoothing with a spatula. Bake 15 to 20 minutes, or until a knife inserted in center comes out clean.

Meanwhile, remove casings from sausage. Crumble meat into a large skillet and cook briefly. Add crushed red pepper and onion. Cook, stirring often, 10 to 12 minutes, or until sausage is cooked through. Drain off fat. As soon as omelet is done, place it on a cooling rack, and then loosen edges all around pan. Grasp edge of paper and pull omelet out onto a cloth towel; invert omelet onto another towel and peel off paper. Sprinkle with cooked sausage and onion, and then scatter Tuscan peppers over top. Evenly arrange cheese slices over all. Quickly roll, starting with a long side. Set on an ovenproof platter and place in oven briefly to melt cheese. Slice and serve immediately. ⤙ Makes 6 servings

1 tablespoon unsalted butter, room temperature

12 eggs, separated

¾ teaspoon salt, or to taste

Pinch of pequín quebrado

1 pound hot Italian sausage

1 teaspoon Italian crushed hot red pepper, or to taste

1 medium onion, thinly sliced and separated into rings

12 or more pickled Tuscan peppers

8 ounces mozzarella cheese, cut in ⅛-inch-thick slices

Pride of Guaymas Shrimp-Avocado Delights

1 ripe avocado, preferably Hass or
    Fuerte variety

1 lime

8 green onions

½ cup mayonnaise

2 tablespoons fresh New Mexico hot green
    chiles, parched (see page 6), peeled,
    seeded, and diced, or to taste

4 slices firm-textured white bread

1 pound cooked, shelled, deveined medium
    shrimp, sliced in half lengthwise

½ cup Margarita Jalapeño Salsa (see page
    128), made without tequila

4 large sprigs fresh cilantro or watercress

Beautiful to behold! Butterflied green onions create a perfect accent for rosy shrimp framed with curving avocado slices and served on toast. This dish is fun and easy to make—and fiesta perfect, combining Mexico's national colors of red, white, and green.

Halve and pit avocado, and then peel each half. Cut lime in half. Squeeze 1 half evenly all over avocado halves. Set avocado halves aside. Trim roots and any wilted tops from green onions. Using a sharp knife, shred top of each onion lengthwise for ⅔ of its length. Cut each of these "butterflied" onions in half lengthwise and set aside.

In a small bowl, squeeze remaining lime half. Blend juice (you need only about a teaspoon) with mayonnaise and chiles. Taste, and add more chiles, if desired. Toast bread. Generously spread each slice with mayonnaise mixture, reserving a little to mix with shrimp. Cut avocado halves lengthwise in ½-inch-thick slices. On each toast slice, place 2 avocado slices facing each other with tips at opposite corners of toast, positioning slices to make an oval. Combine shrimp with remaining mayonnaise mixture and evenly divide among sandwiches, spooning shrimp mixture within avocado slices. Arrange butterflied green onion halves atop shrimp mixture, with white part of onion overlapping avocado and green top extending to corners of toast. Top each sandwich with 2 tablespoons salsa and a cilantro or watercress sprig. Then enjoy! ⇥ Makes 4 servings

Chic Crab Crepes

These are a very special reward for a hard day spent doing anything tedious—or any time you'd like a nice, light, easy-on-the palate treat. At breakfast, serve with luscious drinks; at lunch or late at night, serve with a salad.

In a bowl, beat eggs with a whisk or an electric mixer until fluffy. Beat in milk, 1 ½ cups flour, baking powder, and salt until well blended. (Or process ingredients in a blender until well mixed.) Add 2 tablespoons of the melted butter and mix well. Brush a little melted butter in a well-seasoned 6- to 8-inch crepe pan set over medium heat. When butter is hot, add just enough batter to cover pan bottom, rotating pan to spread batter evenly. When crepe is set on bottom, flip it over and quickly cook other side. Remove from pan. Repeat to cook remaining batter; you should have about 12 crepes. Stack crepes as made, wrap in foil, and keep warm in a 350°F oven.

To prepare sauce, combine remaining melted butter and ⅓ cup flour in a saucepan and cook, stirring, until lightly browned. Add broth and cream, and cook, stirring, until thick and smooth. Stir in cheeses. When cheeses are melted, stir in sherry and a little nutmeg. Keep warm.

In a separate bowl, thoroughly mix crab, bell pepper, celery, and about ½ cup sauce—just enough to make mixture hold together. To fill each crepe, spread a ribbon of crab mixture down center and sprinkle with a little green jalapeño chile. Fold to enclose. Place crepes on ovenproof individual plates or a platter and drizzle with remaining sauce. Sprinkle with red jalapeño or cherry pepper and bake, uncovered, in a 350°F oven for about 10 minutes, or until bubbly.

◁ Makes 4 servings

2 eggs

2 cups milk

1 ½ cups all-purpose flour

1 teaspoon baking powder

Dash of salt

½ cup unsalted butter, melted

⅓ cup all-purpose flour

1 cup double-strength chicken broth

1 cup light cream

½ cup thinly slivered Swiss cheese

2 tablespoons freshly grated Parmesan cheese

2 tablespoons freshly grated Romano cheese

2 tablespoons dry sherry

Freshly grated nutmeg, to taste

½ pound crab meat, drained and all bits of shell removed

½ cup finely diced green bell pepper

½ cup finely diced celery

1 fresh or pickled green jalapeño chile, finely diced

1 fresh or pickled red jalapeño chile or pickled red cherry pepper, finely diced

Jon's Veggie Crepe Cake

3 eggs

1 ¾ cups milk

1 ½ cups all-purpose flour

1 teaspoon baking powder

Pinch of salt

½ teaspoon freshly ground white pepper

1 teaspoon dry mustard

1 teaspoon mustard seeds

1 tablespoon unsalted butter, melted

Vegetable oil

2 cups chopped onions

2 cups coarsely grated Cheddar cheese

2 cups well-rinsed, stemmed, lightly packed fresh spinach leaves

2 cups chopped fresh tomatoes

⅓ cup freshly grated Parmesan cheese

¼ cup minced fresh parsley or 2 tablespoons dried parsley flakes

One of Jon Elben's very favorite brunch dishes is this glorious-looking, French-inspired crepe cake. You can vary the recipe as much as you wish; in fact, Jon says this dish is a wonderfully practical way to use up leftover vegetables, cheeses, sauces—and even meats, if you like. Just be sure to select foods with compatible flavors, colors, and textures. We particularly like this combination.

In a bowl, beat eggs with a whisk or electric mixer until fluffy. Beat in milk, flour, baking powder, salt, white pepper, dry mustard, mustard seeds, and melted butter until well blended. In a well-seasoned 6- to 8-inch crepe pan, heat just enough oil to coat pan bottom (only enough to prevent crepes from sticking). Add a scant ¼ cup batter or just enough to cover pan bottom, rotating pan to spread batter evenly. When crepe is set on the bottom, flip it over and quickly cook other side. Remove from pan. Repeat to cook remaining batter. If made ahead, stack crepes, separating with plastic wrap. Cover and refrigerate for as long as a day.

About 30 minutes before serving, preheat oven to 350°F. Then assemble crepe cake. Lay 1 crepe in a soufflé dish, ovenproof casserole dish, or on a round ovenproof platter. Sprinkle with onions, top with another crepe, and then a layer of Cheddar cheese. Add another crepe, a layer of spinach, a fourth crepe, and a layer of tomatoes. Repeat layers, using remaining crepes, vegetables, and Cheddar. Sprinkle with Parmesan cheese and parsley, and bake, uncovered, for 20 minutes, or until hot and bubbly. ⇥ Makes 4 to 6 servings

Main Meals

Ignited Entrées

EXCITEMENT, INTRIGUE, AND SUSPENSE APTLY DEFINE THE role spice plays in complementing flavor. No matter the source—chiles, ginger, mustard, peppercorns, horseradish, or Wasabi—each enhances the natural flavors of meats, poultry, and seafood.

History is cloudy on just how long humans have sought spice, but one thing is sure: red meat requires more spice to standup to its bold assertive flavors. However, when well-balanced as in the spicy-sweet Hula Steak, the flavor is much more exciting than in the simple sautéed version of the entrée.

Chicken's chameleon-like qualities flavor-wise—absorbing and reflecting the seasonings it captures—are truly enhanced by spicy ingredients. There are an infinite number of ways chicken can become the star of your dinner. Try the Coq au Vin, Caliente, a great classic dish enlivened with crushed red chile, or the Thai-inspired Secret Siamese Chicken, which is as simple and quick to prepare as it is delicious.

Succulent seafood really earns star ratings when spiced up. The mild, slightly sweet flavor of fish and seafood make for terrifically-tempting fare. Try the buttery Sole with Peppered Macadamia Nuts or the Testy Tempura dipped to taste at the table in searing Hot Tempura Sauce.

The best news is that spicy entrées are healthier! It is a proven fact that people eat less of a spicy meal, but get all the healthful benefits, especially if chiles or ginger are used—the two healthiest sources of heat.

Zesty Szechwan Salmon

2 teaspoons cornstarch

2 tablespoons dry sherry

1 tablespoon peanut oil

2 tablespoons fermented black beans

1 teaspoon minced fresh ginger

1 teaspoon minced garlic

⅔ cup chicken broth

1 tablespoon oyster sauce

2 teaspoons dark soy sauce

6 (4-ounce) salmon steaks, cut 1-inch thick

¼ cup vegetable oil

¼ cup thinly sliced green onions (including some green tops)

This flavorful sauce works pure magic on just about any seafood. I especially enjoy it with stronger-flavored fish and seafood—salmon or clams as opposed to sole or shrimp. You can make the sauce ahead and store it in the refrigerator; leftover sauce can be refrigerated indefinitely, too.

Combine cornstarch and sherry, and then add peanut oil, black beans, ginger, garlic, broth, oyster sauce, and soy sauce. Stir until well blended. (Or process ingredients in a blender or food processor until blended.) Set aside.

Prepare a bed of hot coals or preheat broiler. Adjust barbecue grill 4 to 5 inches above coals or position oven rack so fish will be 4 to 5 inches below heat source. Lightly grease barbecue grill or rack in broiler pan. Brush salmon steaks with vegetable oil and place on grill or rack. Cook about 3 minutes, and then rotate a quarter turn and cook 2 to 3 minutes longer to create a crisscross pattern. Turn fish over, and cook other side the same way (total cooking time is 10 to 12 minutes). To check doneness, pierce center of salmon with fork; if flesh is opaque and flakes readily, fish is done. Do not overcook! Place salmon on warmed plates and top each steak with a few spoonfuls of sauce, letting sauce run over sides. Garnish with green onions. ⌁ Makes 6 servings

Hawaiian Sesame Salmon

Vary this simple-to-prepare salmon dish in a myriad of ways—use chopped macadamia nuts, walnuts, or almonds in place of sesame seeds, or top with a favorite hot sauce, such as mustard-dill, pickled pepper, or sweet-and-sour.

Preheat broiler. Beat eggs lightly. Beat in salt and white pepper. In a separate bowl, mix sesame seeds and peppercorns. Dip salmon steaks in egg mixture, then press into sesame seed mixture to coat completely on both sides.

Lightly oil broiler pan, and then arrange steaks well apart in pan. Broil 4 to 5 inches below heat source for 5 minutes, or until browned. Turn and broil 5 minutes longer, or until fish is opaque in center and flakes readily when pierced with a fork. Arrange on a warmed platter. Garnish with lime wedges and serve with hot pepper sauce.

Makes 4 servings

- 2 eggs
- ½ teaspoon salt
- ½ teaspoon freshly ground white pepper, or to taste
- ¼ cup sesame seeds
- 17 whole black peppercorns, coarsely crushed or cracked
- 4 (4-ounce) salmon steaks, cut 1-inch thick
- 4 lime wedges
- Liquid hot pepper sauce

Feisty Tokyo Tuna Steaks

The teriyaki flavor in this dish is enhanced by the spicy wasabi topping. Sushi rice—made by adding white vinegar and sugar to taste—makes a wonderful complement to these steaks.

Blend mayonnaise, red onion, and wasabi in a small bowl, adding more wasabi to taste. Set aside. In a large shallow bowl, combine soy sauce, molasses or brown sugar, garlic, sherry, and vinegar. Add tuna steaks and spoon soy mixture over the tuna. Allow flavors to blend for at least 15 minutes. Turn tuna and spoon sauce over the top. Let rest 15 minutes more.

Brush grill with vegetable oil. Then heat to a medium-high heat. Drain tuna steaks. Grill tuna to desired doneness, about 3 to 4 minutes per side for medium. Top each tuna steak with ¼ of the wasabi topping and serve immediately.

Makes 4 servings

- ⅓ cup mayonnaise
- 1 tablespoon finely chopped red onion
- 1 ½ teaspoons wasabi paste
- 3 tablespoons soy sauce
- 1 tablespoon molasses or brown sugar
- 2 cloves garlic, minced
- 1 ½ teaspoons dry sherry
- 1 tablespoon unseasoned rice vinegar
- 4 (8-ounce) tuna steaks (preferably ahi)
- 1 tablespoon vegetable oil

Turbot Leek Martini

2 large leeks
6 tablespoons unsalted butter
Freshly grated nutmeg, to taste
Freshly ground black pepper, to taste
¾ pound turbot
⅓ cup all-purpose flour
½ teaspoon salt
2 tablespoons minced fresh parsley or
  1 tablespoon dried parsley flakes
2 fresh jalapeño or serrano chiles, finely
  slivered
⅓ cup dry vermouth
Mild red salsa, homemade or bottled, if
  desired
Lemon wedges

Teased with vermouth and slivered hot chiles, delicate-flavored turbot offers a treat for the taste buds—and arranged on a bed of sautéed leeks, it's a feast for the eyes as well. We first enjoyed this dish with a nice bottle of white wine for an al fresco luncheon.

Cut off tops of leeks, leaving about 3 inches of green leaves. Cut leeks in half lengthwise and rinse well, separating layers to wash out dirt. Cut leek halves in long, thin slivers. Melt 3 tablespoons of the butter in a skillet over medium heat. Add leeks. Grate nutmeg generously over leeks, and grind a little pepper over the top. Cook about 5 minutes or until leeks begin to brown. Turn and stir leeks and grate nutmeg and pepper over them again.

While leeks are cooking, melt remaining 3 tablespoons butter in another skillet. Lay turbot out flat. In a small bowl, combine flour, salt, and parsley. Dust turbot evenly with flour mixture. Add turbot to butter and cook, turning once, about 5 minutes per side, or until light golden brown. Sprinkle chiles evenly over fish, pour vermouth into skillet, and quickly bring to a boil. Remove from heat. Arrange leeks spoke-fashion on a platter and set vermouth-coated turbot on top. Garnish turbot with spoonfuls of salsa, if desired, and top with lemon wedges. ⫣ Makes 3 or 4 servings

Sumptuous Swordfish

"Luscious" is the word for this fresh, elegantly-flavored swordfish. Don't compromise on the fresh dill and cilantro, if at all possible. Fresh cilantro is crucial for the flavor; if you can't find it at your regular supermarket, try an Asian grocer or specialty store. Kirby cucumbers are delicious small, tender pickling cucumbers; if they're unavailable, you can use regular cucumbers.

Two hours before planning to serve, combine green onions, orange juice, walnut oil, and 2 tablespoons of the dill in a shallow glass or stainless steel bowl. Place fish in marinade and lightly press into liquid. Turn fish over, and spoon more marinade over top. Let stand at room temperature until ready to cook, turning fish and spooning marinade over top every 15 to 30 minutes.

At least 30 minutes before serving, prepare Salsa de Naranjas. In a medium bowl, combine all ingredients. Let stand at least 30 minutes, tossing and stirring often to blend flavors. Set aside.

To grill fish, prepare a bed of medium-hot coals. Set grill in place about 4 inches above coals; lightly brush grill with vegetable oil. When grill is sizzling hot, place fish on grill, and cook 2 to 3 minutes. Rotate a quarter turn and cook a minute longer to create a crisscross pattern. Turn fish over. Drizzle with some of the marinade and cook 3 to 4 minutes longer, or until fish tests done, rotating a quarter turn after about 2 minutes. To check doneness, insert a knife in thickest part of circular grain of fish; if flesh is moist but not shiny, fish is done.

To serve, place fish on a platter and drizzle with remaining marinade. Spoon a mound of salsa to 1 side of fish. Press remaining 2 tablespoons dill evenly into cucumber slices, and then arrange cucumber slices and orange slices along other side of fish. Top fish with cilantro sprigs.

Makes 4 to 6 servings

3 small or 2 medium green onions, thinly sliced

⅓ cup fresh or reconstituted frozen orange juice

⅓ cup walnut oil

¼ cup minced fresh dill

2 pounds swordfish, cut across the grain

2 tablespoons vegetable oil

8 Kirby or regular cucumber slices

½ orange, unpeeled and thinly sliced

4 to 6 sprigs fresh cilantro

SALSA DE NARANJAS

1 large red-ripe tomato, cut in ¼-inch cubes

Juice of ½ orange

1 teaspoon grated orange peel

4 green onions, thinly sliced

¼ cup coarsely chopped fresh cilantro

2 fresh Oriental hot green chiles, finely minced

Hot Socks Snapper with Olive-Anchovy Topping

¼ cup unsalted butter

¼ cup olive oil

2 large or 4 small cloves garlic, finely minced

4 (6- to 8-ounce) red snapper fillets

½ medium red onion, very thinly sliced and separated into rings

½ cup pimento-stuffed green olives, thinly sliced crosswise

1 tablespoon finely chopped flat anchovy fillets

½ cup fresh jalapeño chiles, parched (see page 6), peeled, and finely chopped (you may substitute pickled jalapeños, but the flavor will not be as fresh)

A sassy topping greatly enhances the mild, moist flesh of snapper—whether red snapper or any other local type. If perchance some "mild mouths" are present among your guests, omit the jalapeños and offer crushed or ground pequín chiles at the table, so those who have a passion for painfully hot foods can please themselves. Do be sure to use only pure chiles for adding at the table, though—commercial "chili powder" just doesn't have the same fresh, fiery-hot flavor.

In a large, heavy skillet, melt butter in oil. When butter is melted and hot, add garlic and let sizzle, but do not allow to brown. Add snapper and reduce heat to medium-low. Cook, turning once, about 5 minutes per side, or until golden brown.

Meanwhile, combine onion, olives, anchovies, and jalapeños. Set cooked fillets on warmed plates, top evenly with olive mixture, and serve warm. ⌁ Makes 4 servings

Double Blue Soft Shell Crabs & Crunchy, Too!

1 cup all-purpose flour

1 teaspoon baking powder

½ teaspoon salt

¾ cup blue cornmeal

3 tablespoons poppy seeds

2 eggs

1 cup milk

¼ to ½ cup unsalted butter

8 small (2- to 3-ounce) soft-shell crabs, washed and cleaned under the shell to remove soft material or 24 large shrimp, peeled and deveined

Margarita Jalapeño Salsa (see page 128)

The rich, nutty flavors of blue cornmeal and poppy seeds beautifully complement sweet, tender crab, and spicy Margarita Jalapeño Salsa adds just the right surprise. Serve with your favorite vegetable side dish and a simple, tartly-dressed salad.

In a bowl, mix flour, baking powder, and salt. Stir in cornmeal and poppy seeds. In another bowl, lightly beat eggs. Blend in milk, and then combine milk mixture with dry ingredients and stir until well blended. Add a little more milk, if necessary, to make a smooth batter that will cling to crabs. Set batter aside.

Melt about 2 tablespoons of the butter in a large, heavy flat skillet, or enough to thinly coat the bottom of the skillet. Dip crabs in batter to coat, add to skillet, and cook until golden on both sides, turning once. Add more butter as you prepare to turn the crabs, adding only enough to keep them from sticking to the skillet. Serve with a side of fresh salsa. ⌁ Makes 4 servings

Huachinango en Salsa Verde

Tart tomatillos are a key ingredient in this luscious, lovely Mexican dish. These little fruits look like green cherry tomatoes with whitish, papery husks—but despite their name and appearance, they're not related to tomatoes. Because fresh tomatillos may be hard to find, I've called for the canned version (available in Mexican markets and some supermarkets). If you can't find canned tomatillos, you may use chopped fresh green tomatoes or even canned red ones—though you won't end up with an authentic Salsa Verde!

To make Salsa Verde, place onion, cilantro, jalapeños, and tomatillos in a blender or food processor and process until very smoothly puréed. Set aside.

    Cut each green chile lengthwise, and open out to make a flat sheet. Set aside.

    Preheat oven to 350°F. Melt butter in a skillet. In a medium bowl, combine flour, salt, and pepper in a shallow, flat-bottomed dish. Dip fillets in flour mixture, and then cook in butter, turning once, about 5 minutes per side, or until light golden brown. Wrap each fillet in a green chile "blanket." Arrange wrapped fillets on an ovenproof platter and top with salsa verde. Place in oven just until salsa and chiles are hot. Serve on warmed plates accompanied by rice.

  Makes 6 servings

½ cup coarsely chopped onion

2 tablespoons chopped fresh cilantro

2 fresh jalapeño chiles, stemmed

1 (13-ounce) can tomatillos, well drained and rinsed

6 fresh green chiles (as hot as you like), parched (see page 6), peeled, seeded, and de-ribbed

About ¼ cup unsalted butter

½ cup all-purpose flour

½ teaspoon salt

Freshly ground black pepper, to taste

6 (6- to 8-ounce) red snapper fillets

Hot cooked rice

Sole with Peppered Macadamia Nuts

¾ cup macadamia nuts

2 tablespoons caribe (crushed Northern
  New Mexico red chile), or to taste

About ¼ cup vegetable oil

8 (6-ounce) sole fillets

2 tablespoons unsalted butter

Juice of ½ lemon

1 tablespoon minced fresh parsley

1 lemon, cut lengthwise in 8 wedges

Note: For those who like it really hot, you can offer additional caribe at the table.

The mild, rich flavors of sole and macadamia nuts take happily to a sassy sprinkle of crushed caribe. If you like, substitute other dried hot red chiles or even finely chopped fresh green jalapeños for the caribe.

Crush macadamia nuts with a rolling pin or chop in a food processor using on-off pulses. Evenly mix nuts with caribe and spread on a large sheet of waxed paper. Heat oil in a large, heavy skillet.

Meanwhile, lightly press both sides of each fillet into nut-caribe mixture, using all mixture and coating each fillet as uniformly as possible. Gently place as many coated fillets in skillet as will easily fit. Cook over medium heat until golden on bottom, and then turn gently, being careful not to break fillets. When second side is golden, turn each fillet out onto a warmed plate and keep warm. Repeat to cook remaining fillets, adding more oil as necessary to prevent sticking. Add butter to nut coating left in skillet. Cook, stirring, until golden brown (do not scorch). Turn off heat and stir in lemon juice. Evenly spoon lemon-butter sauce over fillets.

In a small bowl, mix parsley with sprinkle of caribe. Dust center edge of each lemon wedge with parsley mixture. Garnish fish with seasoned lemon wedges and serve immediately (see Note). Makes 8 servings

Chile-Seared Salmon

A dusting or rub of chile on salmon adds a wonderful flavor. Pan searing or grilling works equally well. If the weather is not conducive to grilling or if you are in a hurry, pan searing is ideal.

In a small bowl, combine the chile, sugar, and salt. Cut the salmon into 2 pieces. Rinse, and then pat dry with a paper towel. Rub the chile mixture evenly over the salmon.

   Add oil to a heavy unseasoned skillet (see Note). Sprinkle with a little salt. Place over medium-high heat until hot. (A sprinkle of water will dance in the bottom of the pan when it is hot.) Sauté the salmon for 3 to 5 minutes per side until crisp and brown on the outside and still moist and bright pink on the inside. Serve on a light pool of salsa.
   ⤎ Makes 2 servings

1 tablespoon ground mild red chile
1 teaspoon sugar
About ½ teaspoon salt
¾ pound fresh boneless salmon fillet
1 tablespoon vegetable oil
1 cup Mango Salsa (see page 126)

Note: If using a seasoned skillet, omit the oil.

Devil's Shrimp

For a super quick, palate-pleasing, devilishly hot dish—serve this! It's great any time, especially on those warm nights when no one really feels like bothering to cook (but everyone who tastes these shrimp will be glad the cook did "bother" a bit).

Melt butter in oil in a large, heavy skillet. When butter is melted and hot, add garlic and let sizzle, reducing heat before garlic starts to brown. Add shrimp and sprinkle with half each of caribe and salt. Cook about 3 minutes, or until shrimp barely begin to turn pink on bottom. Turn shrimp over, sprinkle with remaining caribe and salt, and cook 2 to 3 minutes longer, or until shrimp are pink but still juicy. Taste and adjust seasonings. Sprinkle with cheese, and let stand until cheese starts to melt. Remove coated shrimp to warm plates and serve at once. ⤎ Makes 4 servings

¼ cup unsalted butter
¼ cup olive oil
6 large cloves garlic, finely minced
2 pounds medium shrimp with tails left on, shelled and deveined
2 tablespoons caribe (crushed Northern New Mexico red chile)
1 teaspoon salt, or to taste
½ cup freshly grated Parmesan cheese

Chile-Seared Salmon

Testy Tempura

Tempura is flexible. You can serve it numerous ways, choosing a variety of vegetables, seafood, and/or meat to coat with the delectable batter. A hot, zippy sauce adds extra fun. Here's an assortment of vegetables and shrimp that my friends and family have always liked.

Prepare vegetables and shrimp as noted. (I like to leave the eggplant or zucchini and sweet potato unpeeled, but you may peel them if you wish.) In an electric wok, deep-fat fryer, or deep saucepan, heat about 4 inches of vegetable or peanut oil to 375°F.

When oil is hot and all ingredients are ready, prepare batter. Place flour, cornstarch, and baking powder in a bowl. In a separate bowl, whisk egg yolk and water just until blended. Add to dry ingredients and mix only until blended. Stir in crushed ice. To fry, dip prepared vegetables and shrimp into batter 1 at a time, and then lower into hot oil. Cook only a few at a time to keep batter lacy and to avoid crowding pan. Cook until golden, and then keep warm in a 250°F oven on a paper-towel-lined baking sheet until all pieces are done. Serve warm with Hot Tempura Sauce on the side for dipping. ⇥ Makes 6 servings

1 tiny eggplant, cut in ½-inch cubes or 1 medium zucchini, cut in ¼-inch-thick slices

6 green onions, butterflied (onions left whole, green tops shredded lengthwise with a sharp knife for ⅔ of their length)

2 (¼-inch-thick) slices red onion, separated into rings

6 small spears fresh asparagus

12 sprigs fresh parsley

6 fresh mushrooms, halved

1 medium sweet potato, scrubbed, unpeeled, and cut in diagonal slices

1 pound medium shrimp, shelled, deveined, and butterflied

Hot Tempura Sauce (see page 125)

About 2 quarts vegetable or peanut oil

1 cup all-purpose flour

1 cup cornstarch

½ teaspoon baking powder

1 egg yolk

1 cup cold water

½ cup crushed ice

Sizzling Beer-Batter-Fried Shrimp

¾ cup all-purpose flour

½ cup beer

½ teaspoon salt

1 teaspoon vegetable oil

About 2 quarts vegetable oil

1 egg, separated

1 tablespoon chopped fresh cilantro

1 tablespoon chopped flat-leaf parsley

2 fresh jalapeño chiles, seeded, de-ribbed, and finely minced

1 teaspoon finely chopped chives

1 ½ pounds medium-large shrimp with tails left on, shelled and deveined

HOT BEER MUSTARD

⅓ cup dry mustard

About 2 ½ tablespoons beer

Salt, if desired

A crisp, hearty herb-and-spice coating makes these fried shrimp especially right for any occasion where all the guests have good-sized appetites. I like to serve them after a long day spent out of doors, when the hungry horde won't allow me a lot of time to fuss around in the kitchen! You do have to plan ahead, though. Mix up the batter at least 3 hours ahead and, if possible, clean the shrimp and make the Hot Beer Mustard beforehand, too. French fries and a salad really taste terrific with these shrimp, but you can round out the meal with any dish of your choice.

At least 3 hours ahead of time, prepare batter. Place flour in large, shallow bowl. Stir in beer, salt, and 1 teaspoon oil until smooth. Cover and set aside at room temperature.

When ready to fry, prepare Hot Beer Mustard. Vigorously stir together mustard and beer, adding more beer, if necessary, to achieve desired consistency. Taste, and add a bit of salt, if desired. Set aside.

Then, in a deep, heavy saucepan, heat 4 inches of oil to 375°F. Meanwhile, stir egg yolk, cilantro, parsley, jalapeños, and chives into batter. When oil is hot, beat egg white until stiff, and fold carefully into batter. Dip shrimp into batter, lower into hot oil, and fry until golden. Drain well. Keep cooked shrimp warm in a 250°F oven on a paper-towel-lined baking sheet until ready to serve. Accompany with a side of Hot Beer Mustard. ⊰ Makes 6 servings

Camarones Rancheros

These highly flavorful shrimp make for a terrific party dish, especially since much of the preparation can be done ahead. You can make the sauce early in the day, and then reheat it and cook the shrimp just before serving.

For a spectacular presentation, serve Camarones Rancheros in a rice ring—cook 1 ½ cups long-grain rice according to your usual recipe, but add ¼ cup chopped parsley, 1 clove minced garlic, and 1 cup canned diced chiles. When rice is done, press it into a generously buttered ring mold; if prepared in advance, cover mold and keep warm in a low oven until serving time. To serve, just turn rice ring out onto a platter. A salad of grapefruit sections and onion rings tossed with a honey and poppy seed dressing and served on a bed of lettuce nicely rounds out the meal.

To make sauce, heat ¼ cup oil in a large skillet. Add onions and bell peppers. Cook until onions are clear, but not browned. Add tomatoes and cook only until they are warm and beginning to release their juice. Add jalapeños, salt, and pepper, and simmer briefly—just long enough to blend flavors, but not so long that tomatoes, onions, and bell peppers become overly soft and shapeless. Set aside.

To serve, melt butter in ⅓ cup oil in a large, shallow skillet. When butter is melted and hot, add garlic and cook until slightly golden. Add shrimp and cook quickly, turning as needed, just until shrimp turn pink. Stir in tomato-bell pepper sauce. When sauce is heated, stir in wine and simmer briefly, just long enough to marry flavors.

Meanwhile, pit, peel, and slice avocado. Spoon shrimp mixture over rice or, if desired, into center of rice ring (see recipe introduction). Arrange avocado slices around edge of shrimp mixture and sprinkle parsley over top.

⇥ Makes 6 servings

¼ cup extra virgin olive oil

2 large white onions, thinly sliced and separated into rings

2 large green bell peppers, cut crosswise in thin rings

2 cups peeled, quartered red-ripe tomatoes or 2 cups canned whole tomatoes

3 or more fresh jalapeño chiles, finely minced

¾ teaspoon salt, or to taste

Freshly ground black pepper, to taste

½ cup unsalted butter

⅓ cup extra virgin olive oil

8 to 10 large cloves garlic, minced

3 pounds jumbo shrimp, shelled, deveined, and butterflied

½ cup dry white wine, or to taste

1 ripe Hass avocado

Hot cooked rice

2 tablespoon minced fresh parsley

Red Hot Baby Lobster Tails

8 (4- to 6-inch long) rock lobster tails

½ cup unsalted butter

¼ cup minced green onions (including some green tops)

2 large cloves garlic, finely minced

1 small red radish, finely minced

Juice of 1 lime

2 teaspoons pequín quebrado

1 fresh jalapeño chile, seeded, de-ribbed, and very thinly slivered

1 tablespoon freshly grated Parmesan cheese

1 tablespoon freshly grated Romano cheese

2 teaspoons ground pure California mild red chile

4 large sprigs watercress or other greens

1 lime, cut lengthwise in quarters

Additional pequín quebrado, if desired

These spicy, saucy, succulent lobster tails are flashy both to prepare and to serve. Guests can adjust the heat by drizzling more or less of the peppery-hot butter sauce atop the tails, but even tender-mouthed diners always seem to enjoy the layer of sauce spooned into the shell beneath each tail. Serve as a light entrée, as the fish course for a larger meal, or even as an appetizer.

Preheat broiler. Cut each tail in half lengthwise, using a very sharp knife (leave tails unsplit at back end). Peel meat back off shells. Place tails in a broiler pan and set aside.

Melt butter in a skillet. Add green onions, garlic, radish, lime juice, and 2 teaspoons pequín. Cook, stirring, until garlic is light golden and onions are soft but not browned. Divide ¼ of butter sauce equally among lobster shells, and replace meat in shells. Then evenly divide another ¼ butter sauce among tails, drizzling it over top of each. Sprinkle each tail with jalapeño slivers, cheeses, and some of ground chile. Broil 4 to 5 inches below heat source for about 5 minutes, or until meat is just turning white in center (cut to test).

To serve, place 2 tails on each of 4 warmed plates. Garnish each serving with a watercress sprig and a wedge of lime, lightly rubbing cut edge of lime wedges with ground chile. Offer remaining butter sauce and a small dish of pequín, if desired, for guests to add to their servings as they please.

Makes 4 servings

Pastel de Pescado

Straight from Old Mexico comes this pastry overflowing with the sea's bounty. The quiche-like filling—shrimp, scallops, and lobster in a rich Swiss-cheese custard—nestles in a curved golden crust that's easily made from browned flour tortillas. If you like, you can substitute the catch of the day or any favorite seafood for the choices in the recipe. Serve with a tossed salad and perhaps a vegetable for a wonderful lunch or light supper.

Lightly butter a 9-inch pie plate, using about ½ tablespoon of the butter. Using a sharp knife, cut 3 equal scallop shapes (half moon shapes) off edges of each of 2 tortillas. Melt remaining butter in a medium skillet. Quickly brown remaining whole tortilla, and then the 6 scallop pieces. Place whole tortilla in bottom of buttered pie plate and surround with scallops, forming sides of crust.

Preheat oven to 375°F. Evenly distribute seafood across bottom of tortilla shell. I like to lace shrimp interlocking each other all around outside edge, fill center with scallops, and then lightly scatter lobster or crab over all. Top with garlic and peas.

In a medium bowl, beat together eggs, cream, sherry, salt, and white pepper. Pour evenly over all. Scatter cheese on top. Attractively decorate top of pie: arrange tomato wedges overlapping each other around outside edge, jalapeño slices over tomatoes, and chives in a circle in center. Grate nutmeg over all. Bake 30 to 40 minutes, or until a knife inserted in center comes out clean. Serve warm.

Makes 6 to 8 servings

¼ cup unsalted butter

3 (9- to 10-inch) flour tortillas

18 medium shrimp, shelled, deveined, and tails removed

36 bay scallops (about ½ pound total)

½ pound lobster or crab meat, drained and all bits of shell removed

2 cloves garlic, minced

1 cup fresh peas or 1 cup frozen green peas, thawed

4 eggs

1 cup whipping cream

¼ cup dry sherry

¼ teaspoon salt, or to taste

¼ teaspoon freshly ground white pepper, or to taste

½ cup slivered Swiss cheese

1 tomato, cut in thin wedges

1 or more fresh jalapeño chiles, thinly sliced and seeded

2 tablespoons minced chives

Freshly grated nutmeg, to taste

Cioppino Caliente

¼ cup extra virgin olive oil

1 large onion, chopped

4 cloves garlic, minced

¼ cup caribe (crushed Northern New Mexico red chile)

4 large red-ripe tomatoes, peeled and coarsely chopped

1 (6-ounce) can tomato paste

½ cup Burgundy or other good-quality dry red wine, or to taste

2 teaspoons minced fresh rosemary or 1 teaspoon dried rosemary

1 tablespoon minced fresh thyme

2 bay leaves

2 tablespoons minced fresh basil

1 tablespoon minced fresh oregano

1 teaspoon salt, or to taste

1 pound medium shrimp with the tails left on, shelled and deveined

½ pound king or other crab legs

1 (1 ½-pound) lobster

18 bay scallops (about ¼ pound total)

½ pound firm-fleshed white fish such as cod, cut in 1-inch cubes

12 cherrystone or other small clams, scrubbed

¼ cup dry brandy, if desired

Super hot and so much fun! Served with a warmed loaf of French or Italian bread and a tossed green salad, this robust seafood stew is guaranteed to "wow" your guests. Cioppino is one of my longtime favorite entrées for entertaining. It's best served at intimate, informal dinner parties—preferably with only four diners or even just two!—since it's quite messy to eat.

Heat oil in a large skillet, paella pan, or wok. Add onion and garlic and cook until garlic just starts to turn golden. Add caribe, tomatoes, tomato paste, wine, herbs, and salt. Cover and simmer about 30 minutes, or until flavors are well blended and sauce is somewhat reduced; add a little water if sauce starts getting too thick. Taste and adjust seasonings.

Place all seafood on top of sauce, arranging it in a pretty pattern. Cover and cook 10 to 15 minutes, or until shrimp turn pink, lobster turns red, scallops and fish are opaque, and clams pop open. If desired, quickly heat brandy. Carefully flame and pour over cioppino just before serving.

To serve, divide seafood equally among large, shallow bowls (you'll need to cut lobster apart). Be sure to provide bibs and plenty of napkins! Makes 4 servings

San Francisco Sassy Scallops

A student in one of my Santa Fe Cooking Schools shared this special recipe with me. A former Harvard and Stanford professor who now lives in Woodside, California, he generously told us all how to create one of his favorite appetizer specialties. I'm sure you'll agree it's wonderful!

Place scallops in a glass or porcelain bowl and cover with lemon juice. Stir to coat well. Cover and refrigerate, stirring frequently, about 2 hours, or until scallops "cook" in lemon juice and turn opaque.

   Meanwhile, prepare sauce. In a blender or food processor, process bell peppers, vinegar, oil, pequín, and salt, if desired, until puréed. Taste and adjust seasonings.

   To serve, pit and peel avocado, and then cut lengthwise in slivers. Divide bell-pepper sauce equally among 4 to 6 clear glass plates. Drain scallops, center on sauce, and garnish edge of each plate with avocado slivers.
   ⊰ Makes 3 or 4 servings

1 pound bay scallops
½ cup fresh lemon juice or enough to cover scallops
4 red bell peppers, parched (see page 6), peeled, and seeded
2 tablespoons raspberry vinegar
2 tablespoons extra virgin olive oil
½ teaspoon pequín quebrado, or to taste
Salt, if desired
1 medium Hass avocado

Scallops with Sherried Green Peppercorn Sauce

This fabulously rich, flavorfully sauced dish is surprisingly easy to make and oh, so delicious. It's especially good as a brunch entrée or a late-night dinner. Smaller portions even make an elegant first course.

Melt 2 tablespoons of the butter in a large, heavy skillet over medium-high heat. Add scallops and quickly cook, stirring, until edges are light golden and almost all liquid has evaporated, leaving skillet almost dry. Remove scallops to a platter and keep warm. Add sherry to skillet. Deglaze skillet, and then add cream and cook, stirring, until mixture is reduced by about ⅓. Stir in warm scallops, peppercorns, salt, and caribe. Cook a few minutes, taste, and adjust seasonings. Serve warm in patty shells or over split croissants on warmed plates. ⊰ Makes 4 servings

¼ cup unsalted butter
1 ½ pounds bay scallops
¼ cup dry sherry
½ cup whipping cream
1 (1-ounce) jar pickled green peppercorns, drained
Salt, to taste
1 teaspoon caribe (crushed Northern New Mexico red chile)
4 patty shells or croissants, heated

San Francisco Sassy Scallops

Tia's Favorite Mexican Chicken

Select a very young spring fryer not over 2 ½ pounds, layer it in a pot with fresh vegetables, set it over low heat, and let dinner cook itself. This easy-to-make entrée is straight from the Western ranges; similar dishes were originally prepared over an open fire in heavy cast-iron pots.

Melt butter in a large, heavy pot. Add chicken, skin side down, and cook until browned. Layer on zucchini, squash, bell pepper or poblano, corn, tomatoes, and onions. Sprinkle with garlic and sliced jalapeños. Cover and cook over low heat for 30 minutes. Check periodically; if more liquid is needed, add water or broth. Cover and cook 15 minutes longer, or until chicken and vegetables are tender. Do not overcook. Serve on a warmed platter with vegetables encircling chicken. If desired, offer a dish of chopped jalapeños for the fire-eaters in your crowd. ⊰ Makes 4 servings

¼ cup unsalted butter

1 (2- to 2 ½-pound) young broiler-fryer chicken, cut for frying

1 zucchini, about 6-inches long, sliced

1 yellow crookneck squash, about 6-inches long, sliced

1 large green bell pepper or poblano chile, cut in long, thin strips

4 ears fresh corn, kernels cut off the cob or 2 cups frozen whole-kernel corn

1 pound red-ripe tomatoes, peeled and cut in wedges

2 small onions, thinly sliced

4 cloves garlic, minced

2 or 3 fresh jalapeño chiles, very thinly sliced crosswise

Water or chicken broth

Chopped fresh jalapeño chiles, if desired

Chicken Cutlets with Five Peppers

This dish is so mouthwatering for the ease of preparation! You can make these tender, juicy chicken breasts as fiery or tame as you wish by adjusting the quantity of chiles and pepper you use. Serve with a simple vegetable dish and a crisp salad of your choice.

Brush chicken breasts generously with 1 tablespoon of the oil, and then sprinkle with garlic, rosemary, jalapeños, caribe, and green peppercorns. Press seasonings into meat. Set aside.
    Melt butter in a large, heavy skillet and add remaining 1 tablespoon oil. When oil is very hot, add green and red bell pepper strips and cook until limp. Add chicken. Cook until golden on bottom, turn, and cook until second side is golden and meat is no longer pink in center. Serve on warmed plates. ⊰Makes 4 servings

2 whole (1 ¼-pound) chicken breasts, skinned, boned, split, and pounded very thin

2 tablespoons olive oil

1 large or 2 medium cloves garlic, crushed

2 teaspoons minced fresh rosemary or 1 teaspoon dried rosemary, crushed

3 tablespoons finely minced fresh or pickled jalapeño chiles

3 tablespoons caribe (crushed Northern New Mexico red chile)

1 tablespoon pickled green peppercorns, crushed

¼ cup unsalted butter

1 medium or ½ large green bell pepper, cut in long thin strips

1 medium or ½ large red bell pepper, cut in long thin strips

Winter Chicken-Chile Stew

¼ cup vegetable oil

2 large cloves garlic, coarsely chopped

1 (3 ½-pound) broiler-fryer chicken, cut for frying

6 carrots, peeled and cut in 3-inch lengths

6 medium onions, peeled and quartered

6 medium turnips, peeled and quartered

6 medium potatoes, peeled and quartered

2 large stalks celery, cut in 2-inch lengths

7 cups water

1 teaspoon salt, or to taste

3 sprigs fresh oregano or ½ teaspoon dried oregano

1 fresh bay leaf

6 leaves fresh purple sage or 1 teaspoon dried sage

2 tablespoons ground pure New Mexico hot red chile

1 cup dry white wine

Caribe (crushed Northern New Mexico red chile), if desired

Though it's delightful any time, this stew is perfect for cozy, chilly winter evenings. It's great comfort food, combining the soothing qualities of chicken soup with the hearty surprise of a rosy, chile-sparked sauce laced with dry white wine. If you like, offer spicy caribe at the table for the daring to add at will.

Heat oil in a large, heavy pot, add garlic, and cook just until heated. Add chicken pieces and cook until browned on all sides, turning as needed. Remove from pot. Add carrots, onions, turnips, potatoes, and celery. Cook, stirring, until slightly browned on edges. Return chicken pieces to pot, placing them on top of vegetables. Add water, salt, oregano, bay leaf, sage, ground chile, and ¾ cup of the wine. Bring to boil, reduce heat, cover, and simmer 45 minutes to 1 hour, or until chicken and vegetables are tender. Taste and adjust seasonings. Serve hot, laced with remaining ¼ cup wine. If desired, offer a small bowl of caribe on the side for those who wish to add extra heat. ⊰ Makes 6 to 8 servings

Spicy Summer Chicken Stir-Fry

3 whole (1 ¼-pound) chicken breasts, skinned, boned, and cut in 1-inch-long strips about ½-inch wide

¾ teaspoon salt, or to taste

3 tablespoons unsalted butter

1 small onion, sliced and separated into rings

2 or 3 cloves garlic, minced

2 (6-inch long) zucchini, thinly sliced

2 (6-inch long) yellow crookneck squash, thinly sliced

6 fresh New Mexico hot green chiles, parched (see page 6), peeled, seeded, and chopped

¼ cup chopped fresh cilantro

As summery as a day in June, this medley of light greens and yellows is as flavorful as it is pretty. Serve with the salad of your choice—I like orange or grapefruit slices and red onion rings with a honey and poppy seed dressing.

Sprinkle chicken with salt and stir together. Melt butter in a large wok or very large, heavy skillet over a medium-high heat. Add chicken strips and stir-fry until meat begins to lose its pink color. Push chicken to 1 side, away from hot center of pan. Add onion and stir-fry until it barely begins to get limp. Add garlic, zucchini, and squash. Stir-fry 2 to 3 minutes, or just until color of squash heightens. Add chiles and cilantro. Stir chicken back into center of pan. Stir-fry until chicken is done and squash is still slightly crisp. ⊰ Makes 6 to 8 servings

Coq au Vin, Caliente

This is my all-time favorite coq recipe, developed during my early New Mexico years. Fired with caribe and flamed with cognac, it's a fabulous dish with a perfect marriage of flavors, certain to be a hit with family and guests—though you may want to hoard it all for yourself! Since this stew is so robust, accompany it with a soothing side dish. And never, ever waste a drop of the savory sauce; if you have any leftover, freeze it for later use. It's wonderful in all kinds of stews.

In a paper bag or large, shallow bowl, mix flour, caribe, and salt. Dredge chicken in flour mixture.

Meanwhile, melt butter in a large, deep, heavy skillet (or in a chicken fryer) over medium-high heat. Add chicken pieces and cook until browned on all sides, turning as needed; adjust heat as necessary to prevent over-browning. Add cognac to hot skillet and flame carefully, keeping a lid nearby to extinguish flames should they rise too high. When flames die, stir in garlic, bay leaf, thyme, 3 tablespoons of the parsley, onions, mushrooms, bacon, and a generous grinding of black pepper. Pour wine over all. Bring to a boil, reduce heat, cover, and simmer about 45 minutes, or until chicken is tender and sauce is thickened.

Meanwhile, prepare Fried Croutons. In a skillet, toast French bread cubes in a mixture of half oil and half melted butter until light golden on all sides, stirring as needed. Cool.

To serve, place chicken on a large warmed platter and cover with sauce, arranging onions decoratively around chicken. Sprinkle croutons over the top, and then sprinkle with remaining 1 tablespoon parsley. ⇥ Makes 6 servings

½ cup all-purpose flour

2 tablespoons caribe (crushed Northern New Mexico red chile)

1 teaspoon salt

1 (3 ½- to 4-pound) broiler-fryer chicken, cut for frying

½ cup unsalted butter

6 tablespoons cognac

1 clove garlic, crushed

1 fresh bay leaf

4 sprigs fresh thyme or ½ teaspoon dried thyme

¼ cup minced flat-leaf parsley

6 small white boiling onions, peeled

½ pound fresh mushrooms, thinly sliced

6 thick slices lean, heavily smoked country bacon, cut in ½-inch pieces, partially cooked, and drained

Freshly ground black pepper, to taste

1 cup burgundy or other good-quality dry red wine

FRIED CROUTONS

French bread, cut in 1-inch cubes

Olive oil

Unsalted butter

Phenomenal Pollo

1 (3-pound) broiler-fryer chicken, cut for frying

About 2 cups chicken broth

2 tablespoons juice from pickled jalapeño chiles

1 large onion, quartered

6 to 8 leaves dark green lettuce (Romaine, leaf lettuce, or outer leaves of iceberg lettuce)

½ cup fresh cilantro leaves

1 cup flat-leaf parsley sprigs

1 large clove garlic

6 fresh or pickled jalapeño chiles, stemmed

2 tablespoons extra virgin olive oil (see Note)

1 cup almonds

Salt, to taste

12 (6-inch) corn tortillas, warmed, or 3 to 4 cups hot cooked rice

Guacamole (see page 15), if desired

2 cups sour cream, if desired

Note: For a slightly lower fat and calorie version, reduce the olive oil to 1 tablespoon and the almonds to ⅔ cup—any less affects the flavor and texture.

Subtle and complex in flavor, this Mexican almond chicken in green sauce is elegant enough to serve to company. Don't be daunted by the long list of ingredients; the dish can be made in about an hour. It's absolutely wonderful in warmed fresh corn tortillas with a topping of guacamole and sour cream, or you might also serve it over rice or with a side dish of stewed beans.

Place chicken in a single layer in a large pot. Pour in broth and jalapeño juice. Bring to a boil, reduce heat, cover, and simmer 35 to 45 minutes, or just until tender. Cool in cooking broth. Lift chicken from broth, reserving the broth. Discard skin and bones and tear meat into bite-size pieces.

To prepare sauce, in a food processor or blender, process onion, lettuce, cilantro, parsley, garlic, and jalapeños until quite smooth. Add about 1 cup of the reserved chicken cooking broth, a few tablespoons at a time, until mixture has the consistency of whipping cream. Set aside.

Heat oil in a medium, heavy saucepan and add almonds. Lightly cook and stir over medium-low heat 3 to 5 minutes, or just long enough to slightly toast almonds and heighten their flavor. Add green sauce and cooled chicken and simmer together 10 to 15 minutes, or until flavors are blended and sauce is hot. Taste and adjust seasonings; add salt, if desired. Serve in warmed tortillas or over rice, topped with Guacamole and sour cream, if desired. ⌇ Makes 6 servings

Kentucky's Best Bourbon-Glazed Thighs

This is the gooey, yummy barbecue sauce you think of from the South. The addition of bourbon really makes it special.

Melt butter in large saucepan over medium heat. Add 1 cup onion and cook until clear. Add ketchup, molasses, brown sugar, Worcestershire, mustard, pepper, ground chile, and salt. Reduce heat to simmer until sauce thickens, about 15 minutes. Stir in bourbon, and cook until heated through.

Meanwhile, heat a grill or broiler until hot. Grill chicken until skin is crisp and juices run clear, about 12 minutes per side. When done, brush each side with barbecue sauce and heat in a moderate oven 3 to 5 minutes longer. Transfer thighs to a warmed platter and serve with reserved sauce in a bowl. Garnish with thin lemon and onion slices, if desired.

Makes 4 to 6 servings

¼ cup butter
1 cup onion, finely chopped
1 cup ketchup
¼ cup molasses
2 tablespoons packed brown sugar
1 ½ tablespoons Worcestershire sauce
2 teaspoons yellow mustard
¾ teaspoon ground black pepper
1 teaspoon pure ground hot chile
1 ½ teaspoons coarse kosher salt
⅓ cup bourbon
12 chicken thighs, butterflied to remove bones
2 lemons, thinly sliced, if desired
1 onion, thinly sliced and separated into rings, if desired

Spaghetti Diablo

The devil's own choice! This dish is sprightly and subtly spicy with the potential for real heat, if that's how you like it (just add more pequín). I was given this recipe by Amy White, a Californian I met in Albuquerque.

Butter a 2- to 3-quart casserole dish, using ½ to 1 tablespoon butter. Preheat oven to 350°F. Following package directions, cook capellini in boiling water just until tender to bite. Drain and pour into buttered casserole dish. Set aside.

Melt 2 tablespoons butter in a medium skillet. Add onion, garlic, and mushrooms and cook until onion is limp and slightly golden. Stir tomatoes, salt, pepper, sugar, and pequín into onion-mushroom mixture. Simmer, stirring, for 3 to 4 minutes. Taste and adjust seasonings. Add sauce and cooked chicken to spaghetti in casserole dish. Toss to mix well. Mix cheeses and sprinkle over top. Bake, uncovered, for 20 to 30 minutes, or until cheese is melted and slightly golden. Makes 4 to 6 servings

½ to 1 tablespoon unsalted butter, room temperature
8 ounces dried capellini
2 tablespoons unsalted butter
1 onion, finely chopped
1 clove garlic, minced
1 cup fresh mushrooms, sliced
2 ½ cups peeled, cooked fresh tomatoes
½ teaspoon salt, or to taste
Freshly ground black pepper, to taste
1 tablespoon sugar
1 teaspoon pequín quebrado, or to taste
1 cup diced cooked chicken
¼ cup freshly grated Parmesan cheese
¼ cup freshly grated Romano cheese

Hotter Than Hell Buffet Barbecued Chicken

¼ cup bacon drippings from maple-syrup-
glazed bacon or ¼ cup drippings from
regular bacon plus 1 tablespoon maple
syrup (see Note)

1 cup chopped onion

4 large cloves garlic, minced

1 (44-ounce) bottle ketchup

¼ cup cider vinegar

¼ cup dark molasses

¼ cup Worcestershire sauce

½ cup flat beer

2 tablespoons coarse-grained Dijon-style
mustard

1 tablespoon liquid smoke

1 teaspoon pequín quebrado (or up to 1
tablespoon for really hot sauce)

1 teaspoon freshly ground black pepper

1 tablespoon finely minced pickled
jalapeño chiles (up to 3 tablespoons for
really hot sauce)

2 (3-pound) broiler-fryer chickens, cut for
frying

*Note: For less fat and cholesterol, use 2 tablespoons
vegetable oil instead of bacon drippings. Add 1
tablespoon maple syrup or use ¼ teaspoon maple
extract if maple flavor is desirable.*

The superb spicy sauce that tops this chicken can do wonders for most any meat—and it's party perfect, since its flavor only improves with age. You can just keep reheating the chicken if your guests don't all come to the table at once, as often happens at a swim party, after tennis, and so forth. For a real treat, serve this dish with Red Hot Warm Potato Salad (see page 36).

To make barbecue sauce, melt bacon drippings in a heavy 3-quart or larger pot. Add onion and garlic and cook about 3 minutes. Add ketchup, vinegar, molasses, Worcestershire sauce, beer, mustard, liquid smoke, pequín, pepper, and jalapeños. Stir well, cover, and simmer 30 minutes to combine flavors.

Meanwhile, preheat oven to 400°F. Place chicken pieces, skin side up, in 2 large, shallow roasting pans. Bake 30 to 40 minutes, or until skin is parched. Turn pieces over and reduce oven temperature to 350°F. Generously baste each piece with sauce, using 3 cups of the sauce, and bake 15 minutes longer. Turn again, and baste skin side with pan drippings and 1 cup more sauce. Bake 20 to 30 minutes longer, or until sauce is glazed and tips of chicken pieces are lightly browned. ⌁ Makes 8 to 12 servings

Secret Siamese Chicken

Secret Siamese Chicken

1 tablespoon chopped fresh ginger
2 cloves garlic, finely minced
2 tablespoons dark soy sauce
¼ cup dry sherry
¼ cup vegetable oil
1 whole (1 ¼-pound) chicken breast, skinned, boned, and cut in 1-inch cubes
¼ pound fresh snow peas, cut diagonally in thirds
¼ pound pearl onions, each cut in 3 or 4 thin slices
¼ cup minced fresh basil or 2 tablespoons dried basil, crushed
2 to 4 teaspoons finely minced fresh Oriental hot green chile, caribe (crushed Northern New Mexico red chile), or other hot chile
Hot cooked rice
Hot Hot Oil (see page 123), if desired

Chiles, fresh ginger, and garlic pack a powerful punch in this dish—yet the blend of flavors is surprisingly subtle. If possible, get the tiny, thin, fresh green chiles sold in Asian markets, otherwise, substitute caribe or any other crushed very hot chile. And do be sure to use fresh basil if you can get it.

Combine ginger, garlic, soy sauce, sherry, and 2 tablespoons of the vegetable oil in a shallow glass or stainless steel bowl. Add chicken cubes and stir well. Cover and let stand 30 minutes at room temperature (or refrigerate at least 8 hours), stirring at least twice.

About 10 minutes before serving, heat a wok or very large, heavy skillet until medium-hot, and add 2 tablespoons vegetable oil. When oil is hot but not smoking, drain chicken cubes, reserving marinade. Add chicken to pan and stir-fry about 3 minutes, or until meat has almost lost its pink color. Remove chicken to a warmed platter. Add snow peas, onions, and reserved marinade to pan. Stir-fry about 2 minutes. Turn off heat, and then evenly mix in chicken, basil, and hot chile. Pour onto platter. Serve over rice, and offer Hot Hot Oil to add to individual servings, if desired.

Makes 3 or 4 servings

Double-Mustard-Coated Baked Chicken

¼ cup white wine
¼ cup olive oil
3 tablespoons mustard seeds
3 tablespoons Dijon-style mustard
2 teaspoons freshly ground white pepper
1 tablespoon dried tarragon
2 teaspoons dried dill weed
1 (3-pound) broiler-fryer chicken, cut for frying

With its crunchy, tingly-tart coating of mustard, mustard seeds, pepper, and herbs, this baked chicken is especially great for warm weather. Serve with a pasta salad or a vegetable and thick slices of warm, crisp-crusted bread slathered with butter.

In a blender or food processor, process wine, oil, mustard seeds, mustard, white pepper, tarragon, and dill until well blended. Pour marinade into a large, shallow roasting pan. Roll each piece of chicken in marinade. Let stand at least 30 minutes at room temperature.

Preheat oven to 350°F. Bake chicken in roasting pan with marinade, uncovered, for 1 hour, or until coating is crisp and meat is tender. Baste once after 30 minutes. Serve warm.

Makes 4 servings

Roast Turkey with Garbanzo-Chorizo Stuffing

The flavors of chorizo, garbanzos, and spicy salsa verde complement mild-tasting turkey deliciously. You can cook the garbanzos a day or two in advance; be sure to make the cilantro-laced salsa about an hour before serving.

To prepare Garbanzo-Chorizo Stuffing, cook chorizo in a large skillet over medium-high heat until lightly browned. Drain off all fat and pat chorizo dry on paper towels. Add garbanzos and cook about 15 minutes, or until browned. Remove from heat.

In another skillet, melt butter. Add onions and garlic and cook until onions are soft. Add livers. Cook, stirring, until livers are crisp and brown on the outside. Mash livers coarsely with a fork or potato masher, and combine liver mixture with garbanzo mixture. Stir in parsley, and season with salt. Set stuffing aside.

Preheat oven to 400°F. Rub turkey inside and out with salt. Stuff neck and body cavities with stuffing, and truss with skewers and cotton thread. Set turkey, breast up, on a rack in a roasting pan. Roast 30 minutes. Reduce oven temperature to 300°F. Roast about 4 hours longer, or until skin is golden brown and a meat thermometer inserted in thickest part of thigh (not touching bone) registers 185°F. (Temperature of stuffing should be about 170°F.) During roasting, brush turkey with melted butter every 15 minutes until drippings collect, and then baste with drippings.

About 30 minutes before turkey is done, prepare Salsa Verde. Combine all salsa ingredients in a food processor or blender, and process until smooth. Let stand about 1 hour at room temperature to blend flavors.

When turkey is done, let rest about 25 minutes to let juices settle; then carve. Serve sliced turkey with stuffing and salsa.

⇥ Makes about 15 servings

1 (15- to 17-pound) turkey
1 tablespoon salt
¼ to ½ cup unsalted butter, melted

GARBANZO-CHORIZO STUFFING

1 ½ pounds chorizo, casings removed and
    thinly sliced
2 (15-ounce) cans garbanzos, drained
¼ cup unsalted butter
2 onions, chopped
2 large or 3 medium cloves garlic, minced
1 pound chicken livers, trimmed and
    quartered
1 pound turkey livers, trimmed and
    quartered
2 tablespoons minced fresh parsley
2 teaspoons salt, or to taste

SALSA VERDE

1 pound fresh tomatillos, husks and stems
    removed and steamed over boiling water
    until soft, about 5 minutes
1 clove garlic
4 fresh mild green chiles, parched (see
    page 6), peeled, and seeded or 1 (7-
    ounce) can whole green chiles
1 cup fresh cilantro sprigs
½ onion, chopped

Turkey Mole

About 2 tablespoons vegetable oil

1 ½ pounds turkey thighs or breast

Chicken broth

2 dried poblano or New Mexico chiles, stemmed or ¼ cup ground pure New Mexico hot red chile

1 red-ripe tomato, peeled, seeded, and quartered

8 whole blanched almonds

½ corn tortilla or 3 tortilla chips

½ small onion, cut in chunks

1 tablespoon raisins

4 teaspoons sesame seeds, toasted

1 teaspoon pequín quebrado

¼ teaspoon anise seeds

¼ teaspoon ground cinnamon

¼ teaspoon ground cloves

½ ounce unsweetened chocolate

½ to 1 tablespoon unsalted butter, room temperature

1 lime, cut lengthwise in 6 wedges

A traditional holiday dish in Mexico, often served at Christmas and on other red-letter days, turkey mole is a good choice any time you want a special entrée. My uncle, who lived in Mexico, perfected this mole sauce, and I'm pleased to share his very favorite dinner dish with you.

Heat oil in a large, heavy skillet. Add turkey and cook until browned on all sides, turning as needed. Set skillet aside without washing. Place browned turkey in a saucepan, and add just enough broth to cover turkey. Bring to a boil, reduce heat, cover, and simmer about 1 hour or until turkey is tender. Cool in cooking broth. Lift turkey from broth, reserving broth, and discard skin and bones and tear meat (do not cut) into large chunks. Set aside.

Soak chiles in boiling water to cover until softened. Place chiles and soaking liquid (or ground chile) in a blender or food processor. Add tomato, almonds, tortilla or tortilla chips, onion, raisins, 1 teaspoon of the sesame seeds, pequín, anise seeds, cinnamon, and cloves. Process until smoothly puréed (if using ground chile, add a little hot water as needed). Pour mixture into reserved skillet, and cook over low heat, about 5 minutes, stirring constantly. If mixture seems dry, add a bit of oil. Stir in chocolate and 1 cup of the reserved turkey cooking broth. Stir until chocolate is melted. Taste and adjust seasonings.

Preheat oven to 350°F. Butter a 2-quart baking dish and place turkey in it. Pour mole sauce evenly over turkey, cover, and bake at least 1 hour, or until turkey has absorbed most of the sauce. Stir well after 30 minutes. To serve, sprinkle with remaining 3 teaspoons sesame seeds and encircle with lime wedges. ⊰ Makes 4 to 6 servings

Fiery Mediterranean Roast Pork

These seasonings are so strong, you might be afraid to try this dish—but don't be! The rich, flavorful blend encrusting the roast is savory and magnificent. Serve it with a simple side dish of al dente capellini (thin spaghetti), tossed with sweet butter, olive oil, minced parsley, and Parmesan. For buffet service or a formal presentation, encircle the pork with the capellini.

In a blender or food processor, purée garlic, rosemary, salt, pepper, and caribe. With motor running, slowly pour in oil, and process until a paste forms. Place pork in a roasting pan, bone down, and then coat with rosemary mixture. Let stand at least 2 hours at room temperature to allow flavors to blend.

Preheat oven to 400°F. Roast pork for 15 minutes, and then reduce oven temperature to 325°F. Continue to roast pork 1 ½ hours longer, or until a meat thermometer inserted in thickest part of pork (not touching bone) registers 170°F. Remove from oven and let stand 20 to 30 minutes to let juices settle. To serve, cut in medium-thick slices, cutting straight into bone so each serving will have some of the crust.

⊰ Makes 8 servings

2 heads garlic (approximately 20 to 24 cloves), separated into cloves and peeled

¼ cup chopped fresh rosemary or 2 ½ tablespoons dried rosemary

2 teaspoons salt

2 tablespoons freshly ground black pepper

1 ½ teaspoons caribe (crushed Northern New Mexico red chile)

¼ cup extra virgin olive oil

1 (5-pound) bone-in pork loin roast

Double Cilantro Roast Pork

⅓ cup crushed coriander seeds

1 ¼ cups fine dry bread crumbs

½ cup extra virgin olive oil (see Note)

1 teaspoon freshly cracked black pepper

¾ teaspoon salt, or to taste

1 (3-pound) boneless pork loin roast

1 red bell pepper, cut in small squares

½ cup caribe (crushed Northern New Mexico red chile)

1 cup honey

½ cup fresh lime juice

¼ cup minced fresh cilantro

Note: In testing this recipe to reduce fat, we found that you need at least ¼ cup olive oil to hold the bread crumbs together. The additional amount is needed to keep the crust and roast moist. If low fat is a major concern, then water can be added to the crumbs, using just enough to get the crumbs to hold together. The flavor will not be as rich and the roast will be drier.

This is a grand company dish with the most delightful flavor. Crushed coriander seeds make a crunchy, exotic-tasting coating for the pork. And because the roast is so easy to prepare, you'll have plenty of free time for hosting your party. For an attractive presentation, surround the pork with capellini, drizzle some of the sauce over the pasta, and reserve the rest to spoon over the meat at the table. A tartly-dressed salad and perhaps a vegetable side dish nicely complete the meal.

Combine coriander seeds, crumbs, oil, black pepper, and salt. Mix well. Preheat oven to 400°F. Lay pork roast out flat, inside (cut side) up. Place about ⅓ of crumb mixture on pork, evenly distributing it across surface, and then roll up meat and tie securely in 2 or 3 places with kitchen cord. Place roast, seam side down, on a rack in a shallow roasting pan. Coat with remaining crumb mixture. Roast 15 minutes, and then reduce oven temperature to 325°F. Roast 1 hour longer, or until a meat thermometer inserted in center of meat registers 170°F. Remove from oven, and let stand about 20 minutes to let juices settle.

Meanwhile, prepare sauce. In a small saucepan, combine bell pepper, caribe, honey, and lime juice. Cook, stirring often, for about 15 minutes, or until sauce is slightly thickened and looks somewhat glazed. Remove from heat and mix in cilantro. Serve sauce in a separate bowl to spoon over meat.

Makes about 8 servings

Hot as a Pistol Pulled Pork

Straight from South Carolina, this typical regional barbecue is especially fiery. A slowly grilled pork butt that's pulled into strands for serving in sandwiches, it's vastly different from traditional barbecued ribs basted with a tomato-based sauce—in fact, local feuds have even erupted over which is better! You might enjoy this authentic barbecue served Carolina-style: mix some of the searing-hot pork baste into a bowl of coleslaw, and then tuck the shredded pork into warm, soft, freshly baked buns and top with spoonfuls of the slaw.

Combine vinegar, Worcestershire sauce, pepper, hot pepper sauce, and salt. Mix well. Let baste stand at least 1 hour at room temperature before using. (Never use this sauce as a marinade—it's too hot!)

Meanwhile, prepare grill; it's best to use a covered smoker type. If none is available, you may use any charcoal-type grill, but be sure to cover the pork with heavy foil to equalize the temperature. Since the roast grills for a long time at a low temperature, prepare a large bed of coals. When coals are covered with white ash, spread them out to make a bed. Position grill 5 inches above coals. Let grill heat about 2 minutes, scouring it with a metal brush, if necessary. When grill is hot, set roast in place. Sear 2 to 5 minutes on each side or until uniformly browned, and then brush generously with baste. Close hood and cook 1 to 1 ½ hours, or until meat is tender enough to fall from bone. Turn roast over and baste every 15 minutes. Transfer to a large cutting board. When slightly cooked, use 2 large forks or your hand to pull meat into shreds. Serve as desired or as suggested above.

⤙ Makes 6 to 8 servings

3 cups cider vinegar

2 tablespoons Worcestershire sauce

3 tablespoons finely ground black pepper

2 tablespoons liquid hot pepper sauce

¾ teaspoon salt, or to taste

1 (3-pound) pork butt or shoulder roast

Perky Porky Pigtails

2 tablespoons unsalted butter

2 large cloves garlic, minced

½ pound boneless pork steak, cut in strips 3-inches long and ¼-inch wide

1 tablespoon caribe (crushed Northern New Mexico red chile), or to taste

1 pound dried fusilli (corkscrew spaghetti)

½ cup unsalted butter

½ cup whipping cream

1 cup freshly grated Parmesan cheese

1 tablespoon ground pure California mild red chile

½ cup Italian-style pimento-pepper piccalilli

A distant (and very feisty) cousin of fettuccine Alfredo, this full-flavored dish is one you can never serve often enough—if my family is an indication! They tasted it for the first time when I created it for this book; now, it's one of their favorites. Serve with side dishes of Parmesan cheese and caribe and a crisp green salad with a tart dressing.

Preheat oven to 250°F. Melt 2 tablespoons butter in a heavy skillet. Add garlic and cook until just beginning to turn golden. Add pork strips and cook quickly, turning often, about 5 minutes, or until pork begins to brown. Sprinkle with caribe and continue to cook until meat is quite browned and crisp. Remove from skillet; keep warm in the oven along with 4 to 8 serving plates.

Following package directions, cook pasta in boiling water just until tender to bite. Drain well, return to cooking pan, and cover. In skillet used to cook pork, melt ½ cup butter, add cream, and ½ cup of the cheese. Cook until bubbly, stirring to free browned bits from bottom of skillet. Stir in ground chile, taste, and adjust seasonings. Drizzle sauce over pasta, add pork strips and piccalilli, and toss gently, sprinkling with remaining ½ cup cheese. Continue to stir carefully until well blended. Serve hot on warmed plates.

Makes 4 to 6 servings

Carne Adobada with a Halo of Blue Cornbread

So luscious and unusual! This dish is pretty as a picture, too, with tender pork strips in bright red chile sauce both filling and encircling a ring of blue cornbread layered with two cheeses. Get the pork in the oven first, and then mix up the cornbread and bake it alongside the meat. The pork and cornbread should be done at about the same time.

Preheat oven to 350°F. Combine caribe, water, salt, garlic, oregano, and cumin in a food processor or blender and process until well blended. Pour a little of the chile purée into a 9 x 13-inch baking pan, and then add a layer of pork chops. Add more purée, the remaining chops, and then remaining purée. Cover and bake for 30 minutes. Uncover and bake 30 minutes longer, or until sauce is thickened and meat is fork-tender.

Meanwhile, prepare cornbread. First, generously butter a 9-inch ring mold. Line bottom only of mold with waxed paper. Butter paper. In a large bowl, stir together cornmeal, baking powder, and salt. In another bowl, beat eggs, and then beat in melted butter and sour cream. Combine egg mixture with dry ingredients and stir just until blended. Gently fold in corn. Pour ⅓ of batter into prepared ring mold, and then alternate slices of jack and Cheddar cheese on top of batter. Pour on remaining ⅔ of batter and bake about 45 minutes, or until bread is golden brown on top and a wooden pick inserted in center (not down through cheese) comes out clean. Cool in mold on a cooling rack for 10 minutes.

When pork is tender, remove from oven. Remove and discard bones from chops and cut meat into ½-inch-thick strips. Return meat strips to sauce in baking pan. To serve, gently run a dull knife around edges of cooked cornbread, and then invert onto a platter. Lift off mold and peel off paper. Spoon ⅔ of pork mixture into center of ring, and then spoon remaining ⅓ around ring. Garnish pork mixture with chopped onion. Serve hot. ⊰ Makes 6 to 8 servings

½ cup caribe (crushed Northern New Mexico red chile)

2 cups water

1 teaspoon salt

2 cloves garlic

1 tablespoon ground oregano, preferably Mexican

1 tablespoon ground cumin

2 ½ pounds pork loin chops, cut about ½-inch thick and trimmed of excess fat

1 tablespoon unsalted butter, room temperature

1 cup blue cornmeal

1 ½ teaspoons baking powder

¾ teaspoon salt

2 eggs

⅓ cup unsalted butter, melted

1 cup dairy sour cream

1 (1-pound) can whole-kernel corn, drained

4 ounces Monterey Jack cheese, sliced ¼-inch thick

4 ounces Cheddar cheese, sliced ¼-inch thick

½ cup chopped onion

*Carne Adobada with a
Halo of Blue Cornbread*

Puerco con Chile

The robust flavors of chile and pork marry beautifully in this quick-to-fix dish. You really can use any type of chile. I prefer to use a green chile in the sauce and serve a hotter red chile—as hot as my guests can handle!—alongside the pork strips. Serve Puerco con Chile as a hearty snack, over rice as a main course, or tucked inside a burrito, soft taco, omelet, or crepe.

Dredge pork strips in ground chile or caribe. Melt butter in a heavy skillet, add garlic and green onions, and cook until lightly browned. Push to one side. Add chile-dredged pork strips and cook until crisp and brown. Add green-chile strips. Cook, stirring, for 2 to 3 minutes, or until chiles are warm. Add tomatoes, and cook for 5 to 10 minutes, or until tomato juice begins to cook down. Serve immediately. Accompany with additional caribe on the side, if desired.

⌇ Makes about 4 servings

2 pounds boneless pork shoulder, cut in strips about 2-inches long and ¾-inch thick

1 tablespoon ground pure New Mexico hot red chile or caribe (crushed Northern New Mexico red chile)

¼ cup unsalted butter (see Note)

3 cloves garlic, minced

3 green onions, thinly sliced

6 fresh New Mexico hot green chiles, parched, (see page 6), peeled, seeded, and cut into strips

1 ½ pounds red-ripe tomatoes, peeled and cut in ½-inch-thick wedges

Additional caribe (crushed Northern New Mexico red chile), if desired

Note: For less fat, add only 2 tablespoons of butter to begin, adding more if the pork sticks to the pan.

Lasagna a la Baroque

⅔ pound hot Italian sausages, casings removed and thinly sliced

2 tablespoons Italian crushed hot red pepper

1 teaspoon anise seeds

2 tablespoons unsalted butter

1 cup fresh mushrooms, sliced

2 medium red-ripe tomatoes, peeled and thinly sliced

1 (12-ounce) package wide green lasagna noodles

⅓ cup unsalted butter

⅓ cup all-purpose flour

2 ¼ cups light cream

Salt, to taste

¼ teaspoon liquid hot pepper sauce or cayenne pepper, or to taste

¼ teaspoon freshly ground white pepper, or to taste

Freshly grated nutmeg, to taste

About 1 tablespoon unsalted butter, room temperature

8 ounces thinly sliced mozzarella cheese

½ cup freshly grated Parmesan cheese

After thoroughly enjoying this lasagna in the Baroque Restaurant in New York City ages ago (September, 1967, to be exact), I chased after the chef to get the recipe. Then I spiced it up—and here it is!

Place sausage slices in a heavy skillet and sprinkle with 1 ½ tablespoons of the crushed red pepper. Cook until sausages are lightly browned. Drain off fat and sprinkle sausages with anise seeds. Remove from skillet and set aside.

Wipe out skillet. Melt 2 tablespoons butter in skillet. Add mushrooms and cook until mushrooms are lightly browned and all liquid has evaporated. Add tomatoes, and cook just until tomatoes soften and begin to release juice. Set tomato mixture aside. Following package directions, cook lasagna in boiling water just until tender to bite. Drain cooked lasagna well, rinse in cold water, and set aside.

Meanwhile, prepare cream sauce. Heat ⅓ cup butter in a skillet until light golden, and then stir in flour until well blended. Using a whisk, stir in cream. Whisk until sauce is slightly thickened. Season with salt, hot pepper sauce or cayenne, white pepper, and nutmeg. Remove from heat.

Preheat oven to 375°F. Generously butter a large, shallow casserole dish, about 9 x 13-inches. Layer ingredients in dish as follows: drained noodles, sausage slices, mushroom-tomato mixture, more noodles, mozzarella cheese, and cream sauce. Repeat layers until all ingredients are used, finishing with cream sauce. Sprinkle with Parmesan cheese and dust with remaining ½ tablespoon crushed red pepper. Bake, uncovered, for 30 minutes, or until bubbly.

◄ Makes 6 generous servings

My Favorite Lamb Curry with Condiments

I have worked to perfect this recipe for almost longer than I'd like to admit. I find this particular blend of flavors especially appealing, and it seems to suit everyone else very well, too. Do be sure to use only the very freshest of curry powders, preferably an imported powder (purchased at a specialty shop) or even one that you've made yourself. The grocery-store brands are often terribly stale and contain far too much turmeric.

Dredge lamb in flour, and set aside. Combine garlic, onions, and butter in a very large skillet. Stir over medium heat until onions are lightly browned. Add floured lamb and cook until lightly browned all over, stirring as needed to brown evenly. Add apples, curry powder, brown sugar, raisins, Worcestershire sauce, lemon slices, coconut, black walnuts, lime peel, salt, and water. Bring to a boil, and then reduce heat to low. Cover and simmer about 1 hour, or until meat is fork-tender. Serve curry with rice and your choice of condiments.

◅ Makes 6 servings

3 pounds boneless lamb shoulder, cut in 1 to 1 ½-inch chunks

½ cup all-purpose flour

2 cloves garlic, minced

2 large onions, chopped medium-fine

¼ cup unsalted butter

2 large apples, cored and cut in ½-inch cubes

3 tablespoons curry powder, or to taste

¼ cup packed dark brown sugar

⅓ cup raisins

2 tablespoons Worcestershire sauce

2 lemons, thinly sliced and seeds removed

¼ cup sweetened shredded coconut

¾ cup chopped black walnuts

½ teaspoon grated lime peel

2 teaspoons salt, or to taste

2 cups water

Hot cooked rice

CONDIMENT SUGGESTIONS

Sieved hard-cooked eggs

Chutney

Peanuts

Sweetened flaked or shredded coconut

Raisins

Grated lemon or lime peel

Pineapple chunks

Sliced bananas

Lively Leg of Spring Lamb

Spruce up a leg of lamb with a mustard-herb coating, and serve it with a trio of accompaniments: homemade Jalapeño Jelly, mint jelly, and gravy made from the pan juices.

Using a very sharp knife with a pointed tip, pierce lamb evenly all over. Insert slivers of garlic in slits. Set lamb on a rack in a roasting pan, coat with mustard, and sprinkle with rosemary and pepper or caribe.

 Preheat oven to 425°F. Roast lamb for 20 minutes. Reduce oven temperature to 325°F and roast 2 hours longer, or until a meat thermometer inserted in thickest part of lamb (not touching bone) registers 150°F.

 To serve, remove lamb to a large platter. Let stand about 20 minutes to let juices settle. Meanwhile, sprinkle flour over pan drippings and stir to mix well. Place over medium heat and stir until bubbly. Add enough water to make a smooth, medium-thick gravy. Season gravy with salt and additional pepper or caribe, if desired. Serve lamb with side dishes of jellies and gravy. ⊰ Makes 10 to 12 servings

1 (7- to 8-pound) leg of spring lamb, trimmed of excess fat
2 large cloves garlic, slivered
4 teaspoons Dijon-style mustard
1 teaspoon minced fresh rosemary or ½ teaspoon dried rosemary, crushed
1 teaspoon freshly ground black pepper or caribe (crushed Northern New Mexico red chile)
¼ cup all-purpose flour
Salt
Jalapeño Jelly (see page 127)
Mint jelly

Red, White, and Blue Lamb Chops

Surprisingly flavorful, these patriotic chops are also quite easy to make. Be sure to include the whole new potatoes called for below—they're so delicious with the rich sauce.

Preheat oven to 350°F. Trim excess fat from chops, and then arrange chops in a single layer on a shallow baking pan. Evenly divide caribe among chops, crushing it into both sides of each one. Sprinkle chops with cheese and several grinds of pepper, and then pour broth over all. Bake, uncovered, for 1 ¾ hours, basting generously every 30 minutes.

 Meanwhile, cook potatoes in boiling water for about 20 minutes, or until tender. Drain and arrange around cooked chops. Spoon a lot of pan juices over potatoes, and continue to bake 15 minutes longer, or until chops are fork-tender. Serve sauce separately to spoon over chops and potatoes. ⊰ Makes 4 servings

4 (8-ounce) lamb shoulder chops
2 tablespoons caribe (crushed Northern New Mexico red chile)
4 ounces crumbled bleu cheese
Freshly ground black pepper, to taste
1 cup double-strength beef broth
12 very small thin-skinned potatoes, peeled

Cajun Lamb Chops

2 teaspoons onion powder

2 teaspoons pequín quebrado or cayenne pepper

1 ½ teaspoons garlic juice or powder

1 teaspoon ground thyme

1 teaspoon dry mustard

Freshly ground black pepper, to taste

8 lamb loin chops, cut at least 1 ¼ inches thick

½ cup unsalted butter (see Note)

Note: For lower fat, melt only 2 tablespoons of butter and mix with the spices. Then grill the chops instead of frying.

Inspired by the blackened dishes so popular in Cajun cooking, these chops are spitefully hot and really best when grilled out of doors. If the weather won't permit outdoor cooking, wait for a sunnier day unless you have a really powerful fan above your range to pull out the smoke.

Prepare a bed of very hot coals. Heat a very large, heavy skillet over hot coals or on high heat of range until at the smoking point.

Meanwhile, combine onion powder, pequín or cayenne, garlic juice or powder, thyme, mustard, and several grinds of black pepper. Set lamb chops on a large baking sheet and trim off any excess fat. Melt butter in a small saucepan and brush 1 side of each chop. Evenly divide half the spice mixture among chops, gently rubbing mixture into each. Turn chops over and brush again with butter, and rub with remaining spice mixture. Add remaining melted butter to smoking-hot skillet. Immediately add coated lamb chops, making certain that skillet stays incredibly hot. If skillet begins to cool as you continue adding chops, then cook chops a portion at a time (keep cooked chops warm in a low heat oven, if necessary). Grill very quickly, allowing only 1 to 2 minutes per side. Turn each chop only once and add more butter as needed. Chops should be charred on the outside and still rare on the inside. Serve hot on slightly warmed plates. Makes 4 servings

Peppered Pan-Broiled Beef

Hot, tangy green peppercorns in a rich brandy cream sauce make this a perfect company dish, especially when you don't want to work. You can plan to serve it just 20 minutes after starting to cook (unless, of course, you or your guests prefer well-done beef).

Preheat oven to hottest temperature, about 500°F. Grind white pepper generously over entire surface of beef, and then rub beef with oil and press in rosemary. Melt butter in a large, heavy skillet until smoking hot, and then add beef. Cook quickly, turning as needed, until uniformly dark brown all over. Transfer beef to a baking pan and roast 12 to 15 minutes, or until flesh yields readily when pressed (for rare) or yields slightly when pressed (for medium-rare). If in doubt, pierce meat to center with a sharp knife—if juice is very red, meat is rare.

   While meat roasts, make sauce. Add shallots to butter and meat drippings remaining in skillet and cook until lightly browned. Add broth, mustard, cream, and green peppercorns. Bring to a boil, and boil until slightly reduced. Add brandy and ignite, keeping skillet lid handy to cover flames, if necessary. Continue to reduce sauce, stirring constantly. When beef is done, sauce should have desired consistency. To serve, cut beef in slices, place on individual serving plates, and drizzle sauce over center of slices. ⊰ Makes 4 to 6 servings

Freshly ground white pepper, to taste
2 pounds beef tenderloin
2 tablespoons walnut oil
1 teaspoon dried leaf rosemary, crushed
¼ cup unsalted butter
2 tablespoons chopped shallots
½ cup double-strength beef broth
1 tablespoon Dijon-style mustard
½ cup whipping cream
¼ cup pickled green peppercorns, drained and crushed
⅓ cup dry brandy

Far-Out Filled Flank Steak

1 (2-pound) flank steak
½ teaspoon salt, or to taste
Freshly ground black pepper, to taste
½ cup unsalted butter
2 large onions, chopped
4 cloves garlic, minced
2 eggs, slightly beaten
Milk, if necessary
Ranchero Sauce (see page 129) or
   Margarita Jalapeño Salsa (see page 128)

PEPPERED CORNBREAD

½ cup unsalted butter
1 cup creamed corn
1 cup yellow cornmeal
¼ cup finely chopped, pickled jalapeño
   chiles, or to taste
3 eggs
½ teaspoon salt
½ teaspoon baking soda
¼ teaspoon baking powder
1 cup grated Monterey Jack cheese

Contagiously spicy—each peppery bite of this South American-inspired steak demands another! If some of the cornbread stuffing falls out as you're rolling up the meat, don't despair—just pat it back in with your fingers.

The day before serving or early in the morning, prepare cornbread. Preheat oven to 400°F. Place butter in a 9- or 10-inch cast-iron skillet or baking pan. Set in oven just until melted, but not browned. In a bowl, combine creamed corn, cornmeal, jalapeños, eggs, salt, baking soda, and baking powder. Stir in melted butter and then cheese. Pour into skillet or baking pan and bake for 30 to 45 minutes, or until golden brown. Set aside.

When ready to prepare filled flank steak, crumble cornbread into a 3-quart bowl and set aside. Trim excess fat from steak. If steak is wider than 6 inches across the shortest side, cut in half to make 2 long, slender pieces. Firmly and evenly pound steak as thin as possible. Season with salt and pepper, and set aside.

Melt butter in a very large, flat-bottomed skillet with an ovenproof handle. Add onions and garlic and cook until onions are clear. Using a slotted spoon, lift out half the onion mixture and add to crumbled cornbread. Mix eggs into cornbread mixture, combining well. If mixture seems too dry, mix in a little milk. Spoon cornbread mixture in a long strip down center of steak (or spoon half the mixture down center of each steak half). Roll carefully, picking up any loose pieces of stuffing and patting them back into steak. Secure rolled steak closed with sharp skewers. Add rolled steak to skillet and brown rapidly, spooning remaining onion mixture over sides of steak.

Meanwhile, preheat oven to 350°F. When steak is uniformly browned, spoon Ranchero Sauce or Margarita Jalapeño Salsa over top. Bake in skillet, uncovered, spooning sauce over meat occasionally, 1 to 1½ hours, or until meat is easily pierced to center with a sharp knife and is no longer pink. Cut crosswise in slices to serve.

⊰ Makes 8 to 10 servings

Hula Steak

This steak was a winner at an outdoor barbecue contest! My family and friends really raved about this Polynesian dish. It goes perfectly with Hawaiian drinks, banana or coconut chips, or macadamia nuts. For a dramatic presentation, garnish the steak with a lei of flowers such as petunias or roses.

Mix ginger, garlic, soy sauce, brown sugar, and brandy or bourbon in a shallow dish just large enough to hold meat. Place meat in marinade and turn to coat. Let stand 1 hour at room temperature, turning frequently.

Prepare a bed of hot coals or preheat broiler. Adjust barbecue grill 4 to 6 inches above coals or position oven rack so meat will be 4 to 6 inches below heat source. Brush barbecue rack or broiler pan with a piece of meat fat. Lift meat from marinade, and rub a thin layer of ground ginger on both sides of meat for a spicier, more pungent flavor, if desired. Grill or broil to desired doneness, turning once. Allow 6 to 8 minutes per side for medium-rare. Remove steak to a warmed platter and garnish with a lei, squares of bell pepper, or cubes of pineapple. ⊰ Makes 6 to 8 servings

1 teaspoon ground ginger or 1 (2- to 3-inch) piece fresh ginger, peeled and finely chopped
½ teaspoon garlic powder or 2 cloves garlic, minced
2 cups soy sauce
¼ cup packed brown sugar
¼ cup brandy or bourbon
4 pounds well-aged beef sirloin or other lean, tender, boneless beef steak, cut 1-inch thick

GARNISH SUGGESTIONS
1 lei of flowers
1 large green bell pepper, cut in 1-inch squares
½ fresh pineapple, peeled, cored, and cubed

Peppered Beef Fondue

This fondue is wonderful and surprisingly easy to make. Simply pounding freshly ground pepper into the beef cubes really sets this fondue apart, especially for the "pepper bellies" among us! Buy the best beef you can find and serve with an assortment of your favorite dipping sauces.

Trim any excess fat and gristle from beef, and then cut meat into 1-inch cubes. Crush each side of each cube into pepper, and place beef cubes in a serving bowl. Garnish with parsley sprigs, and refrigerate until ready to cook.

To serve, heat oil to 375°F in a fondue pot, chafing dish, or any electric pan (such as a wok or frying pan). Let guests spear meat on fondue forks and cook in hot oil until as done as desired. Then dunk each piece of cooked meat into dipping sauces. ⊰ Makes 6 servings

1 ½ pounds beef sirloin or other lean, tender, boneless beef steak
¼ cup freshly ground black pepper
Parsley sprigs
2 quarts peanut oil for deep-frying

DIPPING SAUCE SUGGESTIONS
Anchovy butter
Mustard mayonnaise
Barbecue sauce
Dilled horseradish-sour cream sauce

Double-Hot Chile Steaks

½ cup ground pure New Mexico hot red
chile

2 cups canned whole tomatoes or 4 large
red-ripe tomatoes, peeled and quartered

1 cup parched (see page 6), peeled, seeded,
and chopped fresh New Mexico hot
green chiles or 1 (7-ounce) can diced
green chiles

1 red onion, cut in cubes

4 large cloves garlic

½ teaspoon salt

½ teaspoon ground oregano, preferably
Mexican

¼ teaspoon ground cumin

4 pounds well-aged beef sirloin, cut
2-inches thick

One of the heirs to a New Mexico mercantile fortune developed this Albuquerque special. These fiery-hot steaks sort of go with the territory—in New Mexico, they say you can tell the natives by how hot they can handle their chiles! Though it's virtually steaming, the steak sauce is a super complement for the strong flavor of beef.

In a blender or food processor, combine ground chile, tomatoes, green chiles, onion, garlic, salt, oregano, and cumin. Process until puréed. If made ahead, refrigerate until ready to use.

To prepare steak, let both steak and sauce come to room temperature. Then place steak in a shallow dish, coat generously on both sides with sauce and let stand 2 hours at room temperature, spooning more sauce over steak occasionally.

Preheat broiler or prepare a bed of hot coals. Adjust oven rack so meat will be 4 to 6 inches below heat source or adjust barbecue grill 4 to 6 inches above coals. Lightly grease rack in broiler pan or barbecue grill. Broil or grill steak to desired doneness, turning once. Allow 10 to 15 minutes per side for medium-rare. Serve with additional warmed sauce on the side. ⊰ Makes 8 servings

Rosalea's Steak Duncan

This wonderful steak for two comes from the famed Pink
Adobe Restaurant in Santa Fe, New Mexico. Rosalea, owner
and chef, gave me the recipe to pass on to a Texas couple
who attended my Santa Fe Cooking School. They'd tasted
the dish at her restaurant and enjoyed it so much, they
insisted on learning how to prepare it at home! The recipe
calls for 6- to 8-ounce steaks, but for bigger appetites, you
can use bigger steaks—up to 15 ounces each.

Just before preparing the steak, prepare the Green Chile
Sauce (see Tip). Heat oil in a skillet, add onion, and cook
until clear. Stir in green chiles, oregano, coriander or cilantro,
salt, and jalapeño or hot pepper sauce. Cook together about
5 minutes, or until flavors are blended. Remove from heat.
Set sauce aside.

    Trim any excess fat from steaks, and then sprinkle both
sides of each steak with hickory-smoked salt. Set aside.
Preheat broiler or prepare a bed of hot coals.

    Thinly slice mushrooms. Melt butter in a skillet, add
mushrooms, and cook until soft. Keep warm. To prepare
steaks, position oven rack so meat will be 4 to 6 inches below
heat source or adjust barbecue grill 4 to 6 inches above coals.
Lightly grease rack in broiler pan or barbecue grill. Broil or
grill steaks to desired doneness, turning once. Allow 5 to 8
minutes per side for rare, or 7 to 10 minutes per side for
medium. Remove steaks to hot platters, top with mushrooms,
and drizzle with Green Chile Sauce.

  Makes 2 servings

2 (6- to 8-ounce) New York cut prime
  steaks
Hickory-smoked salt
4 large fresh mushrooms
¼ cup unsalted butter

GREEN CHILE SAUCE
2 tablespoons olive oil
1 medium onion, finely chopped
6 to 8 fresh New Mexico hot green chiles,
  parched (see page 6), peeled, seeded, and
  chopped
¼ teaspoon ground oregano, preferably
  Mexican
¼ teaspoon ground coriander or 1 tablespoon chopped fresh cilantro
¼ teaspoon salt
1 teaspoon finely chopped fresh jalapeño
  chile or liquid hot pepper sauce, to taste

*Tip: Serve the Green Chile Sauce over burgers,
chops, chicken, or almost any other dish for a great-
tasting, peppy change from the usual. It's a great
omelet topping, too!*

Rosalea's Steak Duncan

Hot Shot Steaks

These steaks are great for a quick lunch, late-night snack, or even an early-morning breakfast before an active day. They're terrific with a salad and a heap of cottage fries, or with eggs for breakfast.

Very carefully, cut steak in half horizontally to make 2 thin steaks. Trim excess fat from meat, and add fat trimmings to a large heavy skillet and render over high heat. Grind pepper generously over steaks, and then press onion and garlic into steaks. When fat is smoking, add pequín to skillet, sprinkling it very evenly across the surface. Add steaks and sprinkle bell pepper around edges of skillet. Brown steaks quickly on bottom, turn over, and sprinkle with jalapeño slices. Then add bread or roll halves, cut side down, to skillet. Continue to cook until bread is toasted and meat is done to your liking; meat takes only a very short time to cook rare, so watch closely. Serve steaks very hot on grilled bread, and spoon bell pepper along the side. ⨼ Makes 2 servings

½ pound beef sirloin
Freshly ground black pepper, to taste
2 tablespoons chopped onion
2 cloves garlic, finely minced
Generous pinch of pequín quebrado
¼ cup diced red bell pepper
6 or more slices jalapeño chile
1 small loaf French bread or 2 large
  French rolls, split in half

Flaming Fajitas

1 ½ pounds very lean bottom round steak,
  cut ¼-inch thick
1 lime
4 large cloves garlic, pressed
1 to 2 teaspoons pequín quebrado
4 to 6 (12-inch) flour tortillas
¼ cup dry brandy
4 to 6 leaves romaine lettuce, cut crosswise
  in 1-inch strips
Guacamole (see page 15)
Margarita Jalapeño Salsa (see page 128)
  or your favorite Pico de Gallo salsa
¼ cup chopped onion
1 tomato, chopped
⅓ cup chopped fresh cilantro
2 cups sour cream

One of the most popular Tex-Mex foods is the fajita—thinly sliced steak that's pounded and seasoned with lime and garlic, and then quickly grilled and wrapped in a warm flour tortilla. Credit for inventing the dish goes to Mexican workers in the citrus orchards along the Texas border, who grilled shirt steaks this way over open mesquite fires.

Fajitas are traditionally served with Pico de Gallo, an intensely hot salsa, but I prefer to use my own homemade Margarita Jalapeño Salsa. It's an exciting alternative that makes the dish more special. For another twist on tradition, my fajitas are quickly flamed with brandy before serving.

Trim steaks of all excess fat, and then cut into 4 to 6 equal rectangles. Pound steak pieces as thin as possible. Cut lime in half, and squeeze juice over both sides of each piece of steak. Evenly sprinkle steak with pressed garlic and press in pequín. (Pequín quebrado is intensely hot: 2 teaspoons will give a fiery-hot flavor, and 1 teaspoon will get your attention. Use the amount that best suits you and your guests). Stack steaks on a plate and let rest 30 minutes at room temperature.

Prepare a bed of hot coals. Or, if no barbecue is available, heat a large, heavy, well-seasoned cast-iron skillet over high heat for about 20 minutes or until very hot.

Meanwhile, stack tortillas, wrap in foil, and place in a warmed oven. Place 4 to 6 dinner plates in the same oven until warm.

Over the hot coals or in the preheated skillet, quickly grill or pan-grill steaks, turning to sear both sides. Heat brandy in a small saucepan, and carefully ignite. Spoon over steaks. (Keep a large piece of foil or skillet lid at hand; if flames rise too high, just cover them until they subside.) When flames die, place each steak piece in a warm tortilla. Add toppings of lettuce, Guacamole, salsa, onion, tomato, cilantro, and sour cream (or let guests add toppings themselves). Roll gently, folding sides of tortilla to center to cover all fillings. Makes 4 to 6 servings

Bitchy Beef Bourguignonne

Hearty and ornery, this deep-colored, rich-flavored stew is wonderful to make and eat on foggy, rainy days at any time of year. But if you live in a sunny climate, don't wait for bad weather—go ahead and try it. Everybody will love it! Serve it on a bed of thick, flavorful egg noodles or with warm, crusty, fresh French bread oozing with sweet butter.

Combine chopped onion, parsley, thyme, bay leaves, black pepper, green peppercorns, oil, and wine in a 2-quart glass or stainless steel bowl. Stir to blend well. Add beef, stir, and let stand 2 hours at room temperature, stirring occasionally.

Melt 2 tablespoons butter in a large, heavy saucepan. Drain beef cubes, reserving marinade. Add beef to pan. Cook until browned, stirring as needed. Add brandy and flame carefully, stirring it so it ignites well. Add broth and reserved marinade. Bring to a boil, reduce heat, cover, and simmer 2 to 3 hours, or until beef is fork-tender.

Meanwhile, prepare onions. Cut stem and root ends off each. Cook trimmed onions in boiling water for 10 minutes, and then pop onions out of their skins. Melt remaining 2 tablespoons butter in a heavy skillet, and add onions and garlic. Cook until onions are golden brown. Add to stew and simmer at least 30 minutes longer. Taste and add salt, more wine, or other seasonings as desired.

⊸ Makes 6 to 8 servings

1 onion, coarsely chopped

2 tablespoons chopped fresh parsley or 1 tablespoon dried parsley

1 teaspoon dried leaf thyme, crushed

2 bay leaves

2 tablespoons coarsely ground black pepper

2 tablespoons pickled green peppercorns, crushed

2 tablespoons extra virgin olive oil

3 cups burgundy or other good-quality dry red wine

3 pounds beef sirloin, bottom round or London broil, cut in 1-inch cubes

¼ cup unsalted butter

¼ cup dry brandy

2 cups double-strength beef broth

36 small white boiling onions

2 large cloves garlic, minced

Salt, if desired

2 ½ cups red wine, preferably Burgundy
or Zinfandel

3 tablespoons olive oil

1 bay leaf

2 sprigs fresh oregano or 1 teaspoon dried
oregano

4 leaves fresh sage or 1 teaspoon dried sage

2 or more fresh jalapeño chiles, finely
minced

2 ½ pounds beef sirloin or bottom round,
cut in 1-inch cubes

½ cup dried baby lima beans ·

½ cup dried pink or pinto beans

½ cup white navy or pea beans

1 teaspoon salt

4 cups water

¼ cup unsalted butter or olive oil

3 large Italian frying peppers or fresh
poblano chiles, cut in 1-inch strips

2 cups beef broth

1 cup ½-inch squares green bell pepper

1 cup ½-inch squares red bell pepper

1 cup ½-inch squares yellow bell pepper

8 to 12 ounces dried wide egg noodles

Tres y Tres Carne

Three kinds of beans and three colors of bell peppers join
up with tender beef in this rich, robust, flavorful dish.
Though it does require time to make, it doesn't demand
much attention. The stew is truly best if you start with dried
beans; you can cook them while the beef chunks cozy into
the wine-herb marinade, and then just simmer the beef and
beans together slowly to build a rich sauce. Serve over
wide-cut egg noodles, and complete the meal with a fresh
garden or spinach salad.

In a glass or stainless steel bowl, stir together wine, oil, bay
leaf, oregano, sage, and jalapeños. Add beef cubes, stir, and
let stand 2 hours at room temperature, stirring occasionally.

Meanwhile, sort and rinse dried beans, and then place
in a heavy 4- to 5-quart saucepan. Add salt and 4 cups
water. Bring to a boil, cover, turn off heat, and let stand 1
hour. Return to a boil, reduce heat, cover, and simmer
for about 1 ½ hours, or until almost tender, adding more
water as necessary.

In a nonstick or well-seasoned skillet, melt 1 tablespoon
of the butter. Add frying peppers or poblano chiles and cook
until browned. Set aside.

Drain beef, reserving marinade. Melt remaining 3 tablespoons of butter or oil in another heavy nonstick or well-
seasoned skillet over medium heat. Add beef and cook until
lightly browned on all sides. Set aside.

Add browned frying peppers or poblano chiles, browned
beef, and beef broth to saucepan with beans. Cover and simmer 1 to 1 ½ hours, or until beans are very tender and meat
is almost tender. Add bell peppers and simmer 15 to 30
minutes longer, or until peppers and beef are tender.

Following package directions, cook noodles in boiling
water just until tender to bite. Drain well. Mound on a platter
and nestle beef stew in the middle for a very pretty entrée.

⤳ Makes 6 to 8 servings

Sassy Stroganoff

This stroganoff is a tried-and-true favorite spiced up to make a very new and different dish. The beef gets a generous coating of freshly ground black pepper, fresh horseradish, and dry mustard. Serve an optional garnish of chopped jalapeño chiles and caribe on the side for a great party entrée.

Pound pepper into steak strips. Set aside. Melt butter in a large, heavy skillet. Add onion and garlic and cook until onion is lightly browned on edges. Remove from skillet and place in a bowl. Increase heat to high. When skillet is very hot, add steak strips, and cook quickly until browned on outside but still rare on inside. Place on top of onion in bowl, and keep warm.

Following package directions, cook noodles in boiling water just until tender to bite. While noodles are cooking, prepare sauce. Add broth, tomato paste, ground chile, horseradish, and mustard to meat drippings in skillet. Cook over medium-low heat, stirring until well blended. Reduce heat, taste, and adjust seasonings.

Drain noodles and divide among 4 to 6 warmed plates. Immediately stir sour cream and meat-onion mixture into sauce. Heat through and spoon over noodles. Garnish with jalapeños and caribe, if desired. ⇥ Makes 4 to 6 servings

2 tablespoons freshly ground black pepper

1 ¼ pounds beef sirloin or fillet (tenderloin), cut in strips 3-inches long and ¼-inch wide

3 tablespoons unsalted butter

1 large onion, thinly sliced and separated into rings

2 cloves garlic, finely minced

8 ounces dried egg noodles

1 cup double-strength beef broth

2 tablespoons tomato paste

1 tablespoon ground pure New Mexico hot red chile

2 tablespoons freshly grated horseradish

2 teaspoons dry mustard

1 ½ cups dairy sour cream

1 or 2 fresh jalapeño chiles, seeded and finely minced, if desired

2 tablespoons caribe (crushed Northern New Mexico red chile), if desired

Five-Pepper Stir-Fried Beef

½ cup dark soy sauce

1 (1- to 2-inch) piece fresh ginger, peeled and grated

2 tablespoons packed dark brown sugar

¼ cup dry sherry

2 cloves garlic, finely minced

1 ¼ pounds partially frozen beef sirloin or London broil, cut ½-inch thick and thinly sliced

2 tablespoons unsalted butter

¼ cup vegetable oil

1 red bell pepper, cut lengthwise in thin strips

1 green bell pepper, cut lengthwise in thin strips

1 yellow bell pepper, cut lengthwise in thin strips

4 green onions, thinly sliced

1 large leek, rinsed well and cut crosswise in ¼-inch slices (including about 3 inches of leaves)

1 teaspoon caribe (crushed Northern New Mexico red chile)

1 pound fresh spinach, rinsed well

¼ cup sliced pickled red cherry peppers

2 slices capicola (see Note), finely chopped

Hot cooked rice

Note: Capicola is an Italian sausage similar to salami, though not as spicy.

This pretty, flavorful dish is extremely quick to cook, but do be sure to allow ample preparation time for slicing and dicing the vegetables and marinating the meat. Once you start to stir-fry, don't budge from the range—if overcooked, the vegetables will lose their beautiful bright colors. Serve over sushi rice or steamed rice; start the rice cooking before you begin to stir-fry. (You can make sushi rice with a simple mix imported from Japan.)

Combine soy sauce, ginger, brown sugar, sherry, and garlic in a shallow glass or stainless steel bowl. Add beef strips and stir well. Let stand 2 hours at room temperature.

To cook, melt butter and oil in a wok or very large, heavy skillet. When fat is very hot (so that a drop of water quickly sizzles and dances on pan), add bell peppers, green onions, and leek. Sprinkle with caribe, and stir-fry for 5 minutes. Lift beef from marinade, add beef to pan, and stir well. Add spinach, and stir-fry 5 minutes longer. Stir in cherry peppers and capicola, and cook until heated through. Serve over hot rice. ⊰ Makes 4 to 5 servings

Vegetable Dishes

Sizzling Sides

SPICY, SASSY MAIN DISHES call for mild-mannered accompaniments—like those in this chapter. From fluffy whipped Sweet Potatoes Teased with Tequila to Luscious Leeks to crunchy Zucchini Fritters, these side dishes are welcome alongside any extra-hot entrée.

I've included some spicy selections, too, sure to be favored by dedicated fire-eaters as well as those looking for snappy accompaniments to milder main courses. Try Hot Green Beans Vinaigrette, Chile-Cheese Onions, or, for a special treat, sweet-hot Cavolfiore alla Medusa, a wonderful Italian creation.

Luscious Leeks

4 leeks
¼ cup unsalted butter
2 tablespoons packed dark brown sugar
Freshly grated nutmeg, to taste
Freshly ground black pepper, to taste

A soothing dish that goes very well with punishing hot entrées. The sweet caramel coating on the leeks quickly cools down overheated palates.

Rinse leeks very thoroughly, and then cut in half lengthwise. Rinse leek halves, separating layers to wash out dirt. Then cut crosswise in 1-inch-thick slices. Melt butter in a large, heavy skillet over medium heat. Add leeks and sprinkle with brown sugar, several grates of nutmeg, and a generous grinding of pepper. Cook, stirring, until leeks are caramelized on the outside. When edges are as brown as desired, serve.
☙ Makes 6 servings

Sweet Potatoes Teased with Tequila

2 large or 3 medium sweet potatoes (about 2 pounds total)
2 to 4 tablespoons tequila
¼ cup unsalted butter, room temperature
Freshly grated nutmeg, to taste
½ teaspoon salt, or to taste
Freshly ground white pepper, to taste

My daughter Amy has always been able to eat her weight in sweet potatoes. Just for a change, I once added tequila to a favorite recipe instead of the usual orange juice, rum, or brandy. It gave the potatoes a different, interesting taste—and we've been into tequila-sweet potatoes ever since.

Scrub unpeeled sweet potatoes, cut in large chunks, and cook in lightly salted boiling water until tender. Pour off water, cover pan, and let potatoes fluff for about 5 minutes. Quickly peel potatoes and return to pan. Add 2 tablespoons of the tequila, the butter, and nutmeg. Beat with an electric mixer or process in a food processor until smooth. Taste and add salt, white pepper, and 2 more tablespoons tequila, if desired. Serve warm. ☙ Makes 4 to 6 servings

Spicy Yam Soufflé

"Yummy" is definitely the word for this subtle, smooth, and silky soufflé. Much easier to make than the usual soufflé, it is a delightful dish for the simplest or the most elegant affair.

Preheat oven to 350°F. Mash baked yams with milk and butter. Add egg yolks, cheese, salt, nutmeg, and ground chipotles, and mix thoroughly. Beat egg whites until stiff peaks form and fold gently into yam mixture. Place in soufflé dish or oblong bread pan. Bake for 40 to 45 minutes, or until firm to touch. Serve warm. ⌇ Makes 6 to 8 servings

3 cups baked yams
¼ cup butter
¾ cup milk
3 eggs, separated
¾ cup Monterey Jack cheese
½ teaspoon salt
¼ teaspoon fresh nutmeg
1 ½ tablespoons ground chipotles

Mexican Carrots

A tried-and-true favorite in our house, this is one vegetable dish that can be made at a moment's notice, since almost everybody keeps carrots and onions on hand. The Mexican flavor goes nicely with any type of entrée.

Thinly slice each carrot on the diagonal, rolling carrot a quarter-turn after each slice. Set aside. In a large, shallow skillet, wok, or griddle, heat oil over medium-high heat. Add onion and cook briefly. Add carrots, oregano, and pepper. Stir-fry 8 to 10 minutes, or until vegetables are tinged with brown. Serve hot. ⌇ Makes 4 servings

4 large carrots
2 tablespoons olive oil
1 large onion, very thinly sliced and separated into rings
Generous pinch of ground oregano
Freshly ground black pepper, to taste

Zucchini Fritters

This is a soothing side dish that's very welcome with some of the super-hot specials I've included in this book. Quick and easy to make, these fritters are also very appealing even to those who aren't terribly inclined to eat squash of any kind.

Using a food processor or a hand grater, grate zucchini. In a bowl, combine zucchini, onion, garlic, eggs, salt, and chiles. Heat oil in a large, shallow skillet until hot. Drop spoonfuls of zucchini mixture into hot oil, making 2 ½- to 3-inch patties. Cook until browned on bottom, and then turn and brown on other side. Add more oil to pan as needed. Serve hot. ⌇ Makes 4 to 6 servings

4 small to medium zucchini
½ cup finely chopped onion
2 cloves garlic, minced
2 eggs, beaten
Salt, to taste
¼ cup fresh New Mexico hot green chiles, parched (see page 6), peeled, and chopped
About 2 tablespoons olive oil

Spicy Yam Soufflé

Eben's Ever-Special Baked Stuffed Tomatoes

Jon Eben and my husband Brennan have been friends since their bachelor days, when they both sharpened their culinary skills. Jon created these luscious, pretty stuffed tomatoes as a side dish for veal scaloppini, but they're just as good alongside most any grilled meat.

Cut a thin slice from top of each tomato, and then hollow out tomato, cutting out flesh to leave a shell with sides about ¼-inch thick and a top opening about 2-inches wide. Chop tomato flesh (see Note). In the following order, layer garlic powder, Cheddar cheese, mustard, and onion in shells. Top onion with as much chopped tomato as will comfortably fit, and then season with Worcestershire sauce and basil or oregano. Fold each Swiss cheese slice in half, and top each tomato with a folded slice, letting some of it hang over edges. (At this point, you may cover tomatoes and refrigerate up to a day.)

To bake, preheat oven to 350°F. Line a baking pan with foil to keep clean-up to a minimum. Arrange tomatoes on pan, and bake for 15 minutes, or until cheese is bubbly and lightly browned. Serve hot. ⊰ Makes 4 servings

4 medium tomatoes
¼ teaspoon garlic powder
4 (1-inch) cubes Cheddar cheese
4 teaspoons Dijon-style mustard
½ cup chopped onion
4 dashes Worcestershire sauce
1 teaspoon dried basil or oregano, or to taste
4 thin (½-ounce) slices Swiss cheese, each approximately 3 x 6-inches
1 tablespoon chopped fresh chives or parsley

Note: Any leftover chopped tomato can be used in a salsa or as a garnish for burgers, omelets, or salads.

Elote con Queso

I was introduced to this corn custard in childhood by my Mexican Aunt Virginia; it was almost always part of our holiday dinners. The recipe is special in that it's made from fresh corn cut from the cobs—in fact, elote means corn cut from the cob. The custard is delicate, yet rich with cheese and cream, and it is lightly spiced with a hint of green chile.

Preheat oven to 350°F. Butter a 3-quart baking dish. In a food processor, combine corn, baking powder, cheeses, chiles, and sugar. Process just until corn kernels are broken down. In a very large bowl, whisk together eggs and cream. Add corn mixture and stir to combine. Stir in salt. Pour into buttered baking dish. Bake 45 to 55 minutes, or until custard is just set and a knife inserted in center comes out clean. Serve immediately. ⊰ Makes 12 servings

About 1 tablespoon unsalted butter, room temperature
2 ½ cups corn kernels, cut from about 5 ears
1 tablespoon baking powder
8 ounces Monterey Jack cheese, diced
8 ounces Cheddar cheese, diced
4 fresh mild green chiles, parched (see page 6), peeled, and seeded
3 tablespoons sugar
9 eggs
3 cups whipping cream
1 tablespoon salt, or to taste

Chuckwagon Baked Beans

2 (16- to 18-ounce) cans pork and beans or
   1 pound dried beans, cooked as directed
   in recipe introduction
1 cup packed brown sugar
1 teaspoon dry mustard
½ pound salt pork, cut in strips
½ cup ketchup
½ cup chopped green onions (including
   some green tops)

The hearty, satisfying flavor of this dish belies its ease and speed of preparation. It's great with picnic foods or simple grilled meats of any kind, especially when you don't have time to start from dried beans. (If you prefer to cook the beans yourself, boil 1 pound dried white navy or pea beans in about 2 quarts water with 1 ½ teaspoons salt until soft, usually about 3 hours.)

Preheat oven to 350°F. Combine all ingredients and pour into a 2- to 3-quart casserole dish. Bake, uncovered, 2 to 2 ½ hours, or until sauce is thick and beans are dark and crusty on top. If time is short, you may decrease the cooking time to 1 hour, but the beans will not be as tasty.
◄ Makes 8 servings

Quelites

3 tablespoons bacon drippings or lard
½ onion, chopped
2 cloves garlic, minced
3 pounds fresh spinach, rinsed well and
   stemmed
1 teaspoon salt, or to taste
1 pint cherry tomatoes
1 teaspoon caribe (crushed Northern New
   Mexico red chile)

Quelites, or Mexican Greens, are traditionally made with native greens, such as lamb's quarters. Some cooks actually make quite a fuss about using only wild greens, but I've always enjoyed making the dish with spinach or Swiss chard; they're more readily available and taste perfectly delicious. Whichever greens you use, the technique is the same: just stem the leaves, and then stir-fry them in bacon drippings (or other flavorful fat) with onion, garlic, and a hint of caribe. I stir in cherry tomatoes at the end for a colorful accent.

Heat fat in a large skillet. Add onion and garlic, and stir-fry about 5 minutes, or until light golden. Add spinach and stir-fry just until limp. Stir in salt. Remove spinach from skillet with a slotted spoon and keep warm. Add tomatoes to skillet and cook until skins begin to burst. Return spinach to skillet, mix with tomatoes, and stir in caribe. Adjust seasonings and serve immediately. ◄ Makes 12 servings

Naked Chiles Rellenos

Chiles rellenos are most commonly served battered and fried. Relleno simply means stuffed. These are a lot of fun, as they are a takeoff on the traditional rellenos, and, of course, they are not as rich. These rellenos are excellent when served with a grilled steak, pork chops, or chicken.

Preheat the oven to 375°F. Prepare the chiles by stabbing a small hole in each near the top. Combine softened cream cheese and goat cheese. Mix until well blended. Stuff chiles by spooning the soft cheese mixture into the small vent hole. Place on greased baking sheet and bake for 15 to 20 minutes. To serve, place 1 chile on each plate and garnish with lettuce, tomatoes, and olives.

⊰ Makes 4 servings

4 whole green chiles, parched (see page 6) and peeled
4 ounces cream cheese, softened
4 ounces goat cheese (see Note)
3 to 4 leaves iceberg lettuce, shredded
1 small tomato, diced
2 tablespoons sliced black olives

Note: You can use regular-flavored goat cheese, but goat cheese with a Southwest flare is so much better. To make Southwest-flavored goat cheese mix 4 ounces goat cheese together with 1 teaspoon olive oil, ¼ teaspoon pequín, and ¼ teaspoon cumin. Use as directed above.

Chipotle Frijoles

Pintos, the healthiest of all beans, are a palette ready to be painted with flavor, especially spicy flavor. The smokiness of chipotles really enhances the beans' rich flavor. I always prefer the dried chipotles, either stewed and minced or ground. They have a far richer flavor than the canned ones.

Place beans, garlic, and onion in a large pot and cover with water. Cook, uncovered, over medium heat until tender, about 2 hours, watching water level and adding water if necessary to keep beans submerged.

When beans are tender, smash against the side of the pan, add chipotle, oregano, sage, and cumin. Once mixed, add just enough chicken stock to beans to achieve desired consistency and simmer for 30 minutes to blend flavors. If beans are too thick, use chicken stock to thin, do not use water. Just before serving, add salt. Simmer for 1 minute to blend flavors and serve. ⊰ Makes 4 to 6 servings

1 pound dried pinto beans
2 garlic cloves, minced
2 cups coarsely chopped Spanish onion
6 stemmed, dried chipotle chiles, coarsely ground (see Note)
1 teaspoon dried Mexican oregano
1 teaspoon dried sage
1 teaspoon ground cumin
About 3 or 4 cups rich chicken stock
1 teaspoon salt, or to taste

Note: Chipotle chiles are very hot, so if you are not familiar with them, start with 2 chiles and add more to taste.

Cavolfiore alla Medusa

1 large, perfect head cauliflower

¼ cup olive oil

2 large cloves garlic

½ cup piñon nuts

1 teaspoon pequín quebrado or Italian crushed hot red pepper, or to taste

½ cup golden raisins

Salt, to taste

Claudia Medusa spent her childhood in Italy, where she developed a lifelong love affair with Italian cuisine. And what a love it has been—she has turned her knowledge and culinary skill into a successful restaurant and catering company in Woodstock, New York. Claudia says, "The hot, slightly sweet, nutty, crunchy, and tender elements in this cauliflower dish create *una festa per la boca*—a party for your mouth. Leftovers are a great snack, too!"

Set aside some of the light green leaves from base of cauliflower for cooking later. Cut cauliflower into florets (cut rather than breaking to get more uniform pieces). Heat oil in a shallow 10- to 12-inch skillet over high heat. Add cauliflower and cook until lightly golden brown. Add garlic and piñon nuts, and cook until golden brown. Add pequín or crushed red pepper, raisins, and salt, to taste. Gradually stir in a bit of water, adding just enough to steam cauliflower to the al dente stage—tender but still firm to bite. When cauliflower is al dente, reduce heat, toss in reserved leaves, stir, and cover. Continue to cook just until cauliflower stems are tender when pierced and leaves turn brighter in color. Serve hot or cold. ⇥ Makes 6 to 8 servings

Chile-Cheese Onions

2 cups small white boiling onions

1 cup Chile con Queso (see page 14)

Keep this recipe a secret and no one will ever guess how easily you created this wonderfully spicy side dish.

Slice root and stem ends from each onion. Rinse onions, and then cook in boiling water about 15 minutes, or until just tender. Drain and pop each onion of its skin. Rinse cooking pan with hot water, and then add peeled onions and Chile con Queso. Heat through and serve.
⇥ Makes 4 to 6 servings

Snappy Snow Peas

Stir these flavorful snow peas up any time you want to com-plement a dish that needs additional color or texture—snow peas have an abundance of both.

Sliver green onions Japanese-style—trim roots and any wilted tops from onions, and then cut each in 2-inch lengths. Cut onion pieces lengthwise in thin slivers. Set aside.

    Heat oil in a wok or large, shallow skillet. Add snow peas, green onions, ginger, and bell peppers. Stir-fry 3 to 4 minutes, sprinkle with soy sauce, and continue to cook until hot and just barely tender-crisp. Sprinkle with ground chile, stir to mix, and serve hot. ⌐ Makes 4 servings

4 green onions

3 tablespoons vegetable oil

2 cups fresh snow peas, ends and strings removed

1 (1-inch) piece fresh ginger, peeled and very finely minced

¼ to ½ green bell pepper, cut lengthwise in slivers

¼ to ½ red bell pepper, cut lengthwise in slivers

¼ to ½ yellow bell pepper, cut lengthwise in slivers

2 teaspoons light soy sauce

1 teaspoon ground pure New Mexico hot red chile, or to taste

Spicy Calabacitas

Try this dish in the summer, when you can find teensy, tiny finger-sized summer squash still with blossoms attached. You'll love it! If you want to make this side dish into an entrée, just add 2 cups browned ground beef, taco meat, or roast beef slivers and toss together.

Melt butter in a large, heavy skillet. Add onion and garlic, and cook until lightly tinged with brown. Add squash and tomatoes. Stir-fry rapidly, sprinkling with chiles, caribe, salt, oregano, and cumin. Cook just until squash are tender-crisp to bite and brighter in color. Sprinkle with cheeses, turn off heat, cover pan, and let cheeses melt. Then serve warm.
    ⌐ Makes 4 to 6 servings

¼ cup unsalted butter

½ cup chopped red onion

2 cloves garlic, minced

4 cups baby summer squash (yellow crook-neck and zucchini with blossoms attached)

2 large red-ripe tomatoes, peeled and cut into wedges

4 fresh New Mexico hot green chiles, parched (see page 6), peeled, seeded, and chopped

2 tablespoons caribe (crushed Northern New Mexico red chile)

1 teaspoon salt, or to taste

¼ teaspoon ground oregano, preferably Mexican

¼ teaspoon ground cumin

¾ cup coarsely grated Monterey Jack cheese

¾ cup coarsely grated Cheddar cheese

Snappy Snow Peas

Hot Green Beans Vinaigrette

This sassy side is fun to serve as a salad or vegetable with just about any entrée! I sometimes substitute tiny new potatoes for half the beans. (It's not necessary to peel the potatoes entirely—just pare a strip around the center of each potato.)

Snap off ends of beans. In a saucepan, bring water and salt to a boil. Add beans, cover, and cook 5 minutes, or until brighter in color and tender-crisp to bite. Drain, and then immediately add oil, vinegar, jelly, and lime juice. Stir to coat and serve at once. ⫶ Makes 4 servings

1 pound fresh green beans
2 cups water
½ teaspoon salt
2 tablespoons extra virgin olive oil
1 tablespoon wine vinegar
1 tablespoon Jalapeño Jelly (see page 127)
1 teaspoon fresh lime juice

Triple Mustard-Coated Potatoes

Brennan and I first tasted these potatoes in Atlanta at the home of our good friend Nathalie Dupree. They are delicious served with chicken or almost any other meat—and they'll hold for hours in the oven (the flavor even seems to improve on standing). You can alter the recipe to suit your taste by using different types of mustard.

Peel off a thin strip of skin around center of each potato. Cook potatoes in boiling water until tender. Drain, return to cooking pan, and add butter. Cover pan and let stand 5 minutes, or until butter is melted. Stir potatoes to coat with butter. Add pepper, Dijon-style mustard, dry mustard, and mustard seeds, and mix lightly. Place in an ovenproof dish and keep warm in a 150°F oven until serving. Sprinkle with parsley before serving. ⫶ Makes 4 servings

2 cups (about 18) tiny new potatoes, scrubbed
¼ cup unsalted butter, cut in small pieces
Freshly cracked black pepper
2 tablespoons hot Dijon-style mustard
1 teaspoon dry mustard
3 tablespoons mustard seeds
2 tablespoons minced fresh parsley

Wild Rice Baked with Almonds & Mushrooms

½ cup unsalted butter
½ pound fresh mushrooms, thinly sliced
1 clove garlic, finely minced
1 tablespoon minced green bell pepper
½ cup slivered almonds
1 cup uncooked wild rice
3 cups chicken broth
1 teaspoon salt
Freshly ground black pepper, to taste

This recipe was given to me by the chef at a famous resort in Ruidosa. It's extremely easy to prepare and goes well with red meat and all types of game. If you don't have almonds or mushrooms, just substitute other nuts or vegetables of your choice.

Preheat oven to 350°F. Melt butter in a large saucepan. Add mushrooms, garlic, bell pepper, almonds, and rice. Cook, stirring, until mushrooms are soft. Pour mixture into a large, shallow baking dish. Stir in broth, salt, and pepper. Cover and bake about 1 ½ hours, or until rice is tender.
⫷ Makes 6 servings

Middle Eastern Orange-Glazed Carrots with Cumin

3 tablespoons olive oil
Zest of 1 orange
1 ½ pounds medium carrots, peeled and
   cut diagonally into ⅓-inch-thick slices
¾ cup fresh orange juice
¼ cup lime juice
1 tablespoon brown sugar
3 cloves garlic, minced
1 teaspoon cumin
½ teaspoon pequín quebrado, optional
Salt, to taste
Freshly ground black pepper, to taste

Carrots really take to citrus and are much more interesting than when just simmered in water. Searing the vegetables also enhances the flavor, which is emboldened by the addition of the cumin and pequín.

Heat olive oil in large, heavy skillet over medium-high heat. While oil is heating, zest the orange before juicing. Add half the zest, the carrot slices, orange juice, lime juices, sugar, garlic, cumin, and pequín. Bring liquid to a simmer. Reduce heat to medium. Cover and simmer until carrots are crisp-tender, about 5 minutes. If there is too much liquid, reduce juice by simmering over medium-high heat until liquid thickens slightly. Season carrots to taste with salt and pepper. Transfer carrots to bowl, garnish with remaining orange zest, and serve immediately. ⫷ Makes 4 to 6 servings

Condiments and Sauces

Spice it Up!

CHANGE THE PREDICTABLE TO THE PLEASURABLE with spicy, imaginative sauces, relishes, oils, and seasonings. Their origins ranging from the Far East to the Southwest, the favorites presented in this chapter add exciting flavor to a variety of dishes. Hot Salt, Texas Fire Rub, Hot Hot Oil, and more—all are easy to prepare and well worth the small effort involved. And many make wonderful presents from your pantry. Ribbon-tied glasses of Jalapeño Jelly, for example, will delight your friends at holiday time—and even if you've never attempted jelly-making before, you'll find it so simple and so much fun!

Hot Salt

1 tablespoon dried Szechwan peppers
¼ cup kosher or sea salt

This easy-to-prepare condiment offers a great alternative to hot mustard or oil when you want to add some fire to Chinese food. Sprinkle it over meat and combination dishes, or use it as a dipping salt. The tiny, reddish-brown Szechwan peppers, encased in flower-like, star-shaped husks, are sold in Asian markets and spice shops.

Preheat oven to 325°F. Crush peppers slightly by processing briefly in a blender, and then spread on a baking sheet and toast 5 to 10 minutes, or until color deepens and aroma heightens. Combine with salt. Store in the refrigerator.
❧ Makes ¼ cup

Hot Hot Oil

2 cups soybean or other vegetable oil
1 ½ cups caribe (crushed Northern New Mexico red chile)—for hot oil; pequín quebrado—for very hot oil; or tiny dried Chinese hot red chiles—for painfully hot oil

Note: Asian cooks typically allow the chiles to blacken in the oil. I feel that this results in stronger, less fresh-tasting oil, so I recommend removing the oil from the heat before the chiles blacken.

Ouch! If you make this oil hot enough, it really can cause long-lasting pain. When dried chiles are mixed with vegetable oil, their own volatile oils—the source of chile heat—are quickly drawn out and dispersed throughout the oil, ready to cling to the taste buds of the unwary. Nonetheless, Hot Hot Oil is a terrific table condiment for those who take hot foods seriously, as well as a great appetizer dip for bland vegetables and seafood (such as jicama and scallops). You can make the oil just plain hot to painfully hot, depending on the chiles you use.

Mix oil and caribe, pequín, or chiles in a small, heavy saucepan. Warm until oil almost begins to bubble, and then reduce heat; caribe, pequín, or chiles should not turn black (see Note). (If you do not have a good source of low, controlled heat and a heavy saucepan, heat oil first, and then add 1 bit of caribe, pequín, or chile. If it floats and keeps its redness, add the rest. Cover and watch carefully, stirring occasionally.) Cook over low heat until caribe, pequín, or chiles darken but do not turn black. Cool overnight at room temperature, and then strain oil through cheesecloth. Store tightly covered in the refrigerator. Let warm to room temperature to serve. ❧ Makes 1 ½ cups

Hot Pepper Butter

A very convenient condiment to keep at the ready in the freezer, this spread heightens the flavor of meat, seafood, poultry, and vegetables. For extra-hot butter, use caribe rather than ground chile.

In a food processor, process all ingredients until well blended, adding enough wine to give mixture a soft consistency. (Or beat together with an electric mixer.) Use immediately, or shape into a log on a double layer of waxed paper and freeze until firm and then seal in a plastic bag. To use, just cut off a slice of butter and place atop food. (These round pats of butter make a very attractive topping; you might also sprinkle the butter with minced parsley.) Makes 1 cup

2 tablespoons ground pure New Mexico hot red chile or caribe (crushed Northern New Mexico red chile)
1 cup unsalted butter, room temperature
¼ teaspoon fresh lime juice
About 1 tablespoon dry white wine

Bold Bleu Cheese Butter

Flavored butters are a terrific way to add juiciness and complement the flavor of meat. I like to make up this butter and roll it in waxed or parchment paper and keep it in the freezer. I can then slice off a portion and place on top of any steaks, pork chops, grilled chicken breast, or even hamburgers. You can use this recipe as a guide and create your own favorites with nuts, mushrooms, and other favorite flavors instead of the cheese.

Preheat oven to 350°F. Place each garlic head on a separate square of aluminum foil. Lightly drizzle oil over each head, rubbing it onto the skin of the garlic. Loosely wrap foil around each head. Bake for 35 to 45 minutes, or until very soft.

When garlic is cool enough to handle, cut off root area about ¼ inch above the actual root. Place head of garlic on a cutting board and, using a blunt knife, squish the garlic out of the head. Place garlic and remaining ingredients in a food processor and blend together. Place on a 12-inch square of waxed or parchment paper and roll the butter into a log. Roll tightly in the paper and freeze for use anytime.
 Makes about 1 cup

2 heads garlic
1 teaspoon cooking oil
¾ cup butter, softened to room temperature
½ cup bleu cheese, crumbled
3 tablespoons Italian flat leaf parsley, minced
1 tablespoon caribe (crushed Northern New Mexico red chile)

Hot Tempura Sauce

½ cup mirin (sweet sake) or dry sherry
½ cup soy sauce
1 (1-inch) piece fresh ginger, peeled and
  finely grated
¼ pounds daikon, peeled and finely grated
  (see Note)
2 green onions, thinly sliced
Wasabi, to taste

*Note: I often add only 2 ounces daikon to the sauce,
and then batter-fry the remainder (in spoonfuls)
along with the other tempura vegetables.*

This zesty sauce is perfect on almost any batter-fried seafood, poultry, or vegetable. If you like, let your guests temper the sauce's heat: serve extra wasabi (green Japanese horseradish paste) on the side to be blended to taste into individual servings of dipping sauce.

Combine all ingredients and mix well. Serve at once with extra wasabi on the side. Makes about 1 ½ cups

Barbecue Rub

½ cup ground pure, hot or mild red chile
½ cup salt
½ cup dehydrated onion flakes
½ cup dehydrated garlic flakes
¼ cup granulated sugar

This rub is a long-time favorite in the South and West, and especially in Texas, for flavoring meat and vegetables for grilling. Stemming from the days when rubs were used to preserve meat, it is a good way to add spice and flavor to foods. Place leftover rub in a freezer bag or jar for use on ribs, steaks, pork chops, chicken, potatoes, and most any vegetable for grilling. Even popcorn is extra fun when flavored with this devil's dust.

Combine all ingredients together and mix well. To apply, place a small amount in a shallow bowl and, using a spoon, sprinkle over surfaces of meat or vegetables. Be sure to only lightly sprinkle, as the flavors are strong. (Never dip your fingers into the entire amount of rub and then rub onto the meat as it will contaminate the excess.)
Makes 2 ¼ cups

Texas Fire Rub

This rub is excellent on steaks and makes a tasty, spicy crust. It is also very good on potatoes and vegetables. Use sparingly and follow instructions under the Barbecue Rub (see page 125) for applying it to foods.

Mix all ingredients in a jar with a tight fitting lid. To use, coat both sides of steaks or chops with rub. Grill on one side until the coating is crispy and charred. Turn and grill until meat is cooked to taste. ⊰ Makes 1 ½ cups

¼ cup finely ground espresso beans
¼ cup ancho chile powder
1 tablespoon dry mustard
1 tablespoon freshly ground black pepper
1 tablespoon kosher or sea salt
1 tablespoon ground coriander
2 tablespoon brown sugar
1 tablespoon dried oregano
2 teaspoons chipotle powder

Very Hot Shrimp Cocktail Sauce

Super-hot and passionate, this sauce is great over any seafood. Make it as painful as you wish by adding more hot pepper sauce or pequín.

Combine all ingredients. Taste and adjust seasonings. ⊰ Makes 1 cup

¾ cup ketchup
½ cup freshly grated horseradish
Juice of ½ lime
Liquid hot pepper sauce, to taste
½ teaspoon pequín quebrado, or to taste

Mango Salsa

The gingery peach flavor of ripe, pungent mangoes is wonderful with any mild-flavored seafood or poultry. You could also serve this as a dipping salsa with jicama or corn chips.

Combine all ingredients and toss together. Allow the flavors to blend for at least 10 to 15 minutes before serving. ⊰ Makes 1 ½ cups

¾ cup fresh mango, chopped into ½-inch cubes
¾ cup diced Spanish onion
¼ cup coarsely chopped fresh cilantro
2 tablespoons balsamic vinegar
1 tablespoon pequín quebrado

Hotter Than Hell Salsa

The name says it all! This hot salsa was designed specifically for the fish or seafood tacos, but it can be served with anything else that needs a kick. Other chiles may be substituted if you desire a milder heat.

Combine all ingredients in a bowl and mix well. Allow to sit at least 1 hour before serving to allow flavors to blend. ⊰ Makes 1 cup

½ cup diced tomato
½ cup diced Spanish onion
1 small habanero, seeded and diced
1 clove garlic, minced
¾ teaspoon salt

Sonoran-Style Chipotle Tomatillo Salsa

1 pound fresh tomatillos

½ cup onion, coarsely chopped

1 ½ dried chipotles, reconstituted (see Note)

2 tablespoons chipotle cooking juice

1 teaspoon salt, or to taste

¼ cup fresh cilantro or Italian flat leaf parsley

Note: To reconstitute dried chipotles in the microwave, place them in a 1-quart glass measuring cup. Add 1 teaspoon vinegar and water to cover. Cover with cellophane wrap and process on high power for 5 minutes, or until the chiles are softened. Reserve any remaining liquid to add to salsa.

Searing the tomatillos makes them sweeter and gives then a more complex taste. The chipotles add a warm, smoky overtone. Serve warm or cold as a dipping salsa or as a sauce with poultry, seafood, or pork.

Wash, husk, and halve fresh tomatillos. Place in a heavy, cold skillet in a single layer. Place over high heat and cook, uncovered, until the tomatillos toward the center become brown. Turn all tomatillos over, remove from heat, and cover with a tight-fitting lid. Allow to steam until soft—at least ten minutes. Add to blender with all ingredients, except cilantro, and blend until puréed. If mixture seems thick, add additional chipotle cooking liquid or water to make desired consistency. Add cilantro and pulse to mix well.
 ⊰ Makes 2 cups

Jalapeño Jelly

3 large, very ripe red bell peppers, cored and seeded

6 to 8 fresh jalapeño chiles, seeded (for a milder flavor, remove ribs and seeds)

1 ½ cups cider vinegar with 5% acidity

6 ½ cups sugar

6 ounces bottled liquid pectin

Serve this jelly all kinds of ways! It's especially good with cream cheese and crackers as an hors d'oeuvre, as a sauce for roasted meat (see lively Leg of Spring Lamb on page 96), and even as an ingredient in meat and vegetable dishes. And homemade jelly is always well received as a gift from your kitchen. For gift-giving, pour the jelly into decorative glasses or goblets and tie a ribbon around each jar. You might even make fabric coverings to fit over the top.

Using a food processor, finely chop bell peppers and jalapeños. Place chopped peppers and chiles in a large saucepan, stir in vinegar and sugar, and bring to a boil. Boil, uncovered, for about 30 minutes, or until mixture is slightly thickened and peppers are clear. Remove thickened pepper mixture from heat and cool about 10 minutes. Stir in pectin, return to heat, bring to a boil, and boil about 2 minutes longer, or until jelly sheets off the edge of a large metal spoon held at right angles above pan. Remove from heat, skim off and discard foam, and immediately pour jelly equally into 5 or 6 hot, sterilized ½-pint jelly glasses. Cool, seal with paraffin, and cover with lids. ⊰ Makes 2 ½ to 3 pints

Margarita Jalapeño Salsa

A splash of tequila makes all the difference in this robust salsa; it has a way of mellowing the searing nature of hot foods. I like this sauce on seafood, chicken, and any kind of chops—pork, veal, or lamb.

Combine all ingredients and let stand at least 30 minutes at room temperature. Taste and adjust seasonings.

Makes about 1 ½ cups

½ cup cubed tomato

½ cup chopped white or red onion

4 or more fresh jalapeño chiles, very finely minced (see Note)

1 clove garlic, minced

½ teaspoon salt, or to taste

¼ cup gold or white tequila

Note: For a milder salsa, remove seeds and ribs from jalapeños before combining with other ingredients.

Great Green Sauce

1 cup unsalted butter

1 cup stemmed, fresh spinach leaves, steamed over boiling water until limp

¼ cup fresh parsley sprigs

2 green onions, chopped

1 tablespoon chopped fresh dill or 1 teaspoon dried dill weed

1 tablespoon chopped fresh tarragon or 1 teaspoon dried tarragon

1 tablespoon chopped fresh basil or 1 teaspoon dried basil

2 fresh New Mexico hot green chiles, parched (see page 6), peeled, seeded, and chopped

Salt, to taste

This sauce is the perfect dunk for any green vegetable—florets of broccoli, zucchini slices, blanched green beans, snow peas, you name it! Serve at room temperature.

Melt butter in a saucepan and keep warm. In a food processor or blender, combine spinach, parsley, green onions, dill, tarragon, basil, and chiles. Process until puréed. Taste and adjust seasonings, adding salt, if desired. Add to butter and cook, stirring, until mixture is heated through and flavors are well blended. If made ahead, refrigerate in a tightly covered jar; warm by holding jar under hot running water before serving. ⊰ Makes 1 ¾ cups

Ranchero Sauce

1 tablespoon olive oil

½ cup chopped onion

¾ cup tomato juice

1 medium tomato, chopped

1 large clove garlic, chopped

½ cup New Mexico green chiles, parched (see page 6), peeled, seeded, and chopped

¾ teaspoon ground cumin

¼ teaspoon ground oregano, preferably Mexican

½ teaspoon salt, or to taste

This sauce is traditionally served over poached eggs atop softly fried corn tortillas, but as a change of pace, I like to perch the eggs on avocado halves or beds of crab or chicken in a casserole. Try the sauce on hamburgers and omelets, too. You can make it hours or even a day ahead of time.

Heat oil in a medium saucepan or small skillet. Add onion and cook until limp. Add tomato juice, tomato, garlic, chiles, cumin, oregano, and salt. Simmer at least 10 minutes, or until flavors are blended. Taste and adjust seasonings. ⊰ Makes 2 cups

Caliente Green Chile Bites

2 cups (12 to 14) green chiles, parched (see page 6), peeled, and cut into bite-sized pieces

2 red jalapeños, minced

2 cloves garlic, thinly sliced

½ cup sugar

½ cup cider vinegar

1 teaspoon dry mustard or mustard seed

½ teaspoon salt, or to taste

These Bites are delicious in a southwestern antipasto assortment, as a topping on bruschetta, or as an ingredient in a quesadilla tortilla wrap.

Place green chiles, jalapeños, and garlic in a sterilized mason jar. In a small saucepan, bring sugar, vinegar, mustard, and salt to a boil. Simmer 5 to 10 minutes. Slowly pour sugar-vinegar mixture over chiles and garlic. Seal tightly and marinate in refrigerator at least 48 hours. ⊰ Makes 1 pint

Beer Garden Spread

This spread is straight from the Bierstuben of Bavaria—but enhanced with horseradish, mustard, and pequín. Serve any favorite seasonal vegetables alongside.

In a food processor, process all ingredients, except vegetables, until smooth. Place in a crock or pottery bowl and refrigerate at least 2 hours, or until firm. To serve, place on a platter, and attractively arrange vegetables around dip. Dunk vegetables in dip or spread dip on vegetables with a knife.
 Makes about 2 cups

8 ounces small-curd cottage cheese

½ cup unsalted butter, room temperature

1 tablespoon caraway seeds

1 tablespoon freshly grated horseradish, or to taste

1 tablespoon dry mustard, or to taste

1 teaspoon pequín quebrado or cayenne pepper, or to taste

1 tablespoon capers

¼ cup chopped onion

1 (2-ounce) can anchovy fillets, undrained and mashed

Fresh vegetables of your choice, sliced or cut in sticks or wedges as appropriate

New Mexico Piccalilli Relish

Perhaps looking for ways to use the zucchini squash cultivated by local Pueblo Indians, the Spanish, English, and German settlers of the Southwest all concocted hot relishes like this one. It's a favorite of several Spanish families in New Mexico.

Stir together zucchini, chiles, onions, and salt in a large bowl. Let stand 2 hours at room temperature, stirring occasionally. Cover and refrigerate overnight.

The following day, drain and rinse with cold water until water runs clear. Turn into a large saucepan and stir in vinegar, sugar, mustard, celery seeds, and caribe. Bring to a boil, and boil, uncovered, for 30 minutes. Pour relish into 6 hot, sterilized 1-pint canning jars, leaving 1 ½ inches head space. Wipe rims clean with boiling water, and then seal jars tightly with canning lids and rings. Cool filled jars at room temperature out of drafts. Store in a cool, dry place until ready to use. Makes 6 pints

8 cups chopped zucchini

½ cup fresh New Mexico hot green chiles, parched (see page 6), peeled, seeded, and chopped

4 cups chopped hot onions

⅓ cup pickling salt

2 ¼ cups cider vinegar with 5% acidity

4 cups sugar

1 tablespoon dry mustard

1 tablespoon celery seeds

1 tablespoon caribe (crushed Northern New Mexico red chile)

Pickled Jalapeños

15 pounds whole, blemish-free, small to medium fresh jalapeño chiles
2 cups extra virgin olive oil
10 small white onions, sliced and separated into rings
5 large cloves garlic, chopped
5 medium carrots, peeled and thinly sliced crosswise
2 teaspoons ground oregano, preferably Mexican
3 fresh bay leaves
2 tablespoons salt
3 cups distilled white vinegar with 5% acidity
2 ½ cups distilled water

Home-pickled chiles are much prettier and more flavorful than the commercial variety, and they are really worth the effort. Use them for flavoring sauces, soups, stews, and main dishes—or, if you're very brave, just eat them as is! To speed preparation, you can use a food processor to slice the onions and carrots.

Scrub jalapeños, trimming off stems. Set aside. Into a large, deep, heavy pot, pour ½ cup of the oil (enough to coat the bottom). Heat oil until almost at the smoking point, and then turn off or reduce heat. Add onions, garlic, and carrots. Stir only until onions are clear, making sure not to brown any of the vegetables. Add oregano, bay leaves, and salt, and stir to mix. Add vinegar and water and bring to a boil, stirring often. Continue to boil and stir until salt is dissolved, and then add remaining 1 ½ cups oil. Return to a boil. Stir in jalapeños and remove from heat. Fill 16 to 20 hot, sterilized 1-pint canning jars, leaving 1 ½ inches head space. Wipe rims clean with boiling water, and then seal jars tightly with canning lids and rings. Cool filled jars at room temperature out of drafts. Store in a cool, dry place until ready to use.
⌁ Makes 16 to 20 pints.

Jalapeño Hollandaise

3 egg yolks (see Note)
1 to 2 tablespoons fresh lime juice
½ cup unsalted butter, melted
¼ teaspoon salt, or to taste
2 or 3 fresh jalapeño chiles, parched (see page 6), peeled, seeded, and finely chopped
Generous pinch of caribe (crushed Northern New Mexico red chile)

Note: For best results, use the yolks of large, very fresh eggs. And to add extra flavor, stir in chopped fresh basil leaves before serving.

The snappy sharpness of jalapeños and the tang of fresh lime juice give this popular sauce a heated edge. Spoon it over poached eggs, as in eggs Benedict, or serve it with asparagus, broccoli, artichokes, or other favorite green vegetables.

In the top of a double boiler, beat together egg yolks and 1 tablespoon of the lime juice. Drizzle in about ⅓ of the melted butter in a thin stream, and then set over boiling water. Add remaining melted butter in a thin stream, beating constantly. Continue to beat until thickened, adding salt and jalapeños. Taste and add 1 tablespoon more lime juice, if desired. Spoon sauce over foods of your choice. Garnish with caribe and serve. ⌁ Makes ⅔ cup

Beverages

Douse the Flame

COOLING BEVERAGES OFFER THE PERFECT RELIEF for hot days and hard work, and the perfect start for a spicy meal. I've selected an assortment of my favorite drinks here—some newly created, some tried and true. You'll find coolers such as Summer Heat, featuring vodka and Midori; the Vicious Vaquero, a high-octane blend of tequila, caribe, Chartreuse, and ice; and classics like Margaritas and Silkies. When tequila is called for, the best ones to use are those distilled from all-natural agave plants—check the label.

If you're looking for soothing after-dinner drinks, you'll find those, too. Try a creamy Pink Mermaid or perhaps the Gulf Stream Gulp. And to warm up chilly days, my own New Mexican Hot Chocolate can't be beat. It's spicy, frothy, and extra-special—almost rich enough for dessert!

One note of caution: Don't make the mistake of drinking a lot of cold beverages to cool your scorched palate during a spicy meal. You'll just prolong the pain. Instead, turn to the comfort of dairy products like sour cream, butter, and cheese.

Maria's Martinis

2 ounces or more top-quality gin or vodka
Dry vermouth, to taste (most people like a
sparing splash)
4 ice cubes
1 pickled jalapeño chile

These elegant drinks are so easy! Just prepare your favorite martini recipe, and spice up the garnish.

In a cocktail shaker, combine gin or vodka, vermouth, and ice cubes. Shake until thoroughly chilled. Strain into a stemmed cocktail glass or serve on the rocks in an old-fashioned glass. Garnish with a jalapeño. ⚔ Makes 1 serving

Dante's Downfall

1 ounce Grand Marnier
6 whole pink, white, or black peppercorns

This flaming after-dinner drink is delightfully different from the usual cordials and liqueurs.

Pour liqueur into a heatproof snifter or Irish coffee mug. Add peppercorns. Heat by tilting and rotating over a candle or gas flame until the first bubble forms, and then carefully ignite with a match and serve flaming. ⚔ Makes 1 serving

Mexico City Madman

Ice cubes
1 ½ ounces light tequila
1 ½ ounces 151-proof rum
Splash of green Chartreuse
1 lime wedge

After two or more of these daring drinks, you'll hear mariachis in the distance!

Fill a double-old-fashioned glass with ice cubes, and then add tequila, rum, and Chartreuse. Stir. Squeeze lime wedge over drink, stir, and serve immediately. ⚔ Makes 1 serving

Fen's Fang

4 fresh or canned pineapple chunks
1 tablespoon cream of coconut
1 (2-inch) piece fresh ginger, peeled
1 ounce light tequila
1 ounce light rum
½ ounce crème de almond
½ teaspoon frozen orange juice concentrate
About 1 cup cracked ice or 6 to 8 ice cubes
1 fresh daisy or other flower, if desired
1 maraschino cherry

Fen, a sophisticated Canadian stockbroker friend of ours, specializes in this Polynesian cooler with a south-of-the-border influence. It's a pretty melon color with the true taste of the tropics.

Combine 2 of the pineapple chunks, cream of coconut, ginger, tequila, rum, crème de almond, orange juice, and ice in a blender. Process until foamy. Pour into a glass and garnish with a flower, if desired. Add remaining 2 pineapple chunks and a maraschino cherry. ⚔ Makes 1 serving

Blanco Burro

This luscious drink is as beguiling as a burro. Even though it looks very gentle, it can really deliver a kick!

Place 6 to 8 ice cubes in a cocktail shaker, and then add Cointreau, Chartreuse, and cream. Shake well, and strain into an old-fashioned glass. Add more ice cubes to fill glass. Gently sprinkle glass with red hots. ⫞ Makes 1 serving

Ice cubes
1 ounce Cointreau
1 ounce green Chartreuse
1 ounce whipping cream
6 candy red hots

Son of a Bitch's Delight

If you like stingers, you'll like this good-tasting drink. Watch out, though—it's strong.

Fill a double-old-fashioned glass to the rim with ice cubes. Add brandy, bourbon, vodka, and crème de menthe. Stir vigorously. Garnish with mint. ⫞ Makes 1 serving

Ice cubes
1 ½ ounces brandy
1 ½ ounces bourbon
1 ½ ounces vodka
¾ ounce white crème de menthe
1 mint sprig

Gulf Stream Gulp

This drink is as sea green, foamy, and refreshing as a newly beached wave. You might be tempted to gulp—but you're best off sipping.

Fill a cocktail shaker with ice and pour in Sambuca and Chartreuse. Vigorously stir or shake until foamy. Serve in a snifter or pony glass. ⫞ Makes 1 serving

About 1 cup shaved ice
1 ounce Sambuca
2 ounces green Chartreuse

Pink Mermaid

This concoction is cooling, pretty, creamy, and wonderful as an after-dinner drink. If no blender is handy, just crush the ice and then shake or whisk the ingredients together.

Place cream, vodka, crème de almond, and ice cubes in a blender. Process until ice is completely crushed and mixture is frothy and light pink. Pour into a glass and top with brandy. ⫞ Makes 1 serving

2 ounces whipping cream
1 ounce vodka
1 ounce crème de almond
4 to 6 ice cubes
½ ounce brandy

Summer Heat

1 cucumber spear or mint sprig
Ice cubes
2 ounces vodka
½ ounce Midori
1 lime wedge
Club soda

This cool drink is so soothing on searing, sizzling summer days—especially after long hours in the office or a morning's maneuvers on the tennis court.

If using cucumber spear, prepare by cutting a large cucumber in half, and then cut a wedge from cucumber half. Pare off peel in a single flap very close to flesh, peeling halfway up the wedge. Set aside.

Fill a tall, slender 12-ounce glass to the rim with ice cubes, and then add vodka and Midori. Squeeze lime wedge over drink and drip into glass. Add club soda to fill. Stir with a swizzle stick. Hang cucumber spear over edge of glass or garnish drink with mint. If desired, serve with tall, thin straws. ⚔ Makes 1 serving

Silkies

This silky smooth drink is so special that friends have called me from halfway around the world just to get the recipe. This is a great brunch drink, so be prepared to supply a lot of refills!

Place ice cubes, orange juice, lime juice, and tequila in a blender. Process until slushy. Add cream, egg whites, and sugar and process on highest speed until very foamy. Serve in stemmed glasses. ⤞ Makes 4 servings

10 ice cubes

½ cup frozen orange juice concentrate

1 ounce fresh lime juice

4 ounces gold tequila

6 ounces light cream

2 egg whites

3 tablespoons sugar, or to taste

Tracy's White Trash

6 ounces milk
2 ounces Frangelico

This drink has become popular, especially during the winter, at Churchill's—a chic pub on New York's Upper East Side. It was invented by Tracy, one of the pub's veteran bartenders.

Heat milk until steaming. Place Frangelico in an 8-ounce mug and pour in milk. ⤸ Makes 1 serving

Guadalajara Guzzler

Ice cubes
1 ounce light tequila
1 ounce Campari
About 8 ounces club soda
1 thin orange slice
½ thin lime slice
Thin twist of lemon peel

This is a tall, refreshing cooler that's easy to make. The colorful garnish adds to its festive look.

Fill a tall 12-ounce glass with ice cubes. Pour in tequila and Campari, and then fill with club soda. Cut orange slice from edge to center. Lay the half-slice of lime opposite the orange cut and twist the 2 slices together. Attach fruit slices and lemon twist to the end of a wooden pick and garnish drink. ⤸ Makes 1 serving

Vicious Vaquero

2 ounces light tequila
¼ teaspoon caribe (crushed Northern New Mexico red chile)
1 ounce green Chartreuse
6 ice cubes

Note: To make Vicious Vaquero Martinis, garnish each drink with a jalapeño-stuffed olive.

This one is a winner with our friends! It's an unusually good, spicy takeoff on the margarita—truly fit to be associated with the Mexican cowboys.

Combine all ingredients in a blender and process until slushy. Serve immediately (see Note). ⤸ Makes 1 serving

Dona's Death

1 ounce green Chartreuse
1 ounce light tequila
1 ounce Triple Sec
4 ice cubes
1 thin lime slice

Note: To add variety to this drink, add 1 ounce crème de almond to the blender.

Brennan's sister, Dona, likes these cocktails—but she warns, "be careful!"

Combine Chartreuse, tequila, Triple Sec, and ice cubes in a blender and process until well blended (see Note). Pour into a stemmed cocktail glass. Cut a slit in lime slice, and hang on edge of glass. ⤸ Makes 1 serving

Caspar's Cooler

This is a treat from the Old South. Caspar, a devilish Dutchman, gave us the recipe. He concocted this specialty for his close friends, and now he's pleased to share his secret formula with you.

Combine Southern Comfort, vodka, gin, grapefruit juice, orange juice, Grenadine, and ice in a cocktail shaker and shake well. Pour into a tall, slender 12-ounce glass. Fill glass with club soda. Twist orange slice, place grapes in center of slice, and secure with wooden picks. Garnish drink.

Makes 1 serving

1 ounce Southern Comfort
1 ounce vodka
1 ounce gin
3 ounces fresh grapefruit juice
1 ounce fresh orange juice
Splash of Grenadine
1 cup crushed ice
Splash of club soda
1 orange slice, cut just to center
2 green grapes

New Mexican Hot Chocolate

Traditional Mexican hot chocolate is made with Mexican bar chocolate—a mixture of chocolate, sugar, ground almonds, cinnamon, and cloves. My adaptation of the traditional recipe tastes much like authentic Mexican chocolate, but has a better texture. To present your hot chocolate Mexican-style, beat it at the table with a molinillo—a carved wooden stirrer made just for this purpose—and serve it in heavy earthenware mugs. Molinillos are available at specialty kitchenware stores. They're a lot of fun to use and add a bit of showmanship to your presentation!

Combine cocoa, flour, sugar, salt, ground cinnamon, cloves, and water in a heavy 2-quart saucepan. Stir or whisk until very well blended, and then heat just until bubbly around edges and barely beginning to simmer. Gradually add cream and milk in a very thin stream, beating constantly with a molinillo, whisk, or rotary beater. Heat until hot but not boiling. Keep warm for at least 5 minutes. Stir in vanilla.

Just before serving, beat chocolate again with molinillo until frothy. (For a dramatic presentation, do this at the table.) To serve, rinse out 6 mugs with boiling water, and then ladle in hot chocolate. Top each serving with a dollop of whipped cream and a grate of nutmeg. Decoratively place a cinnamon stick into cream. Serve immediately.

Makes 6 servings

⅓ cup unsweetened cocoa powder
1 tablespoon all-purpose flour
⅓ cup sugar
Pinch of salt
¾ teaspoon ground cinnamon
¼ teaspoon ground cloves
1 cup water
2 cups light cream
1 cup milk
1 ½ teaspoons Mexican vanilla extract or
   2 ¼ teaspoons regular vanilla extract
1 cup whipped cream
Freshly grated nutmeg, to taste
6 cinnamon sticks

Margaritas

2 or 3 Mexican or key limes
Coarse salt, if desired
2 ounces Cointreau or Triple Sec
6 ounces light tequila
1 egg white
6 to 8 ice cubes

Note: To serve a crowd more easily and save time, I often mix up Margarita Punch, made with frozen concentrated limeade. Even though the flavor is compromised a bit, you'll still have a much better drink than any commercial mix will yield. Amounts for 6 servings are 10 ounces tequila, 5 ounces Cointreau or Triple Sec, 3 ½ ounces frozen limeade concentrate, and 8 ½ ounces fresh lime juice. Increase amounts as needed.

This is by far the most favored drink for sipping before a spicy-hot meal. The recipe below is our very favorite formula, perfected over the years and guaranteed to get rave reviews. The drink is best made with juice from Mexican or key limes—the small, thin-skinned, yellow-green ones. Substitute the large, dark green Persian limes if you must, but never use bottled or prepared juice.

Roll limes under your palm briefly to bring out the juice. Cut in half and squeeze to make at least ¼ cup of juice. Cover and refrigerate juice.

Rub lime rinds around rims of 2 glasses, preferably stemmed or old-fashioned glasses. Then dust rims with salt, if desired, and freeze glasses for at least 30 minutes to frost them.

To make margaritas, combine cooled lime juice, Cointreau or Triple Sec, tequila, egg white, and ice cubes in a blender. Process until frothy. Serve immediately in the frosted glasses. ⚔ Makes 2 servings (see Note)

Voodoo Punch

¾ cup packed light brown sugar
1 (3-inch) piece fresh ginger, peeled and thinly sliced
2 tablespoons whole black peppercorns
1 tablespoon whole allspice
4 cinnamon sticks
2 cups water
1 large ice block or ice ring (made by freezing water in a 2-quart container of your choice)
1 (750-ml) bottle dark Caribbean rum
1 (750-ml) bottle vodka
2 cups fresh or reconstituted frozen orange juice, or to taste
½ cup pineapple juice, or to taste
10 white or pastel daisies, hibiscus, or other pretty flowers
10 thin lemon slices
Ice cubes

Straight from the Caribbean, this punch is perfect for large parties. Make it when you want the atmosphere to be special— perhaps even a little crazy!

In a 1-quart saucepan, combine brown sugar, ginger, peppercorns, allspice, cinnamon sticks, and water. Bring to a boil, reduce heat, and simmer, uncovered, for 30 minutes. Strain, discarding spices, and allow to cool. If made ahead, set aside until ready to use.

To prepare punch for serving, place ice block or ring in a large punch bowl. Add cooled syrup, rum, vodka, orange juice, and pineapple juice. Taste and add more juices, if desired. Poke stem of each flower through center of a lemon slice. Float lemon slices atop punch. Serve each drink over ice cubes. ⚔ Makes about 32 servings

Desserts

Soothing Sweets

Everybody loves dessert! And if you like your meals hot, you probably know how satisfying soothing sweet desserts can be. Each of the favorites in this chapter is a perfect crown for a super-hot meal. The classic close for a spicy dinner is ice cream, of course—like my dramatic Christmas Cardinale Bombe. Sweet and rich in butterfat, this luscious treats cools overheated palates in a hurry. But you'll find warm desserts, too—Butterscotch Peach Crisp, velvety Dessert Fondue, Steve's Skillet Cake, and many more.

The collection in these pages includes old family favorites as well as recent inspirations. Devil's Food Cake with Fudge Frosting has been in my files since I was 9 years old, but Sumptuous Chocolate-Walnut Soufflé with Cognac-Laced Whipped Cream and Red Raspberry Revel Sauce was created just for this book. Enjoy!

Devil's Food Cake

6 tablespoons unsweetened cocoa powder
1 cup boiling water
1 teaspoon baking soda
¾ teaspoon Mexican vanilla extract or 1
   teaspoon regular vanilla extract
½ cup solid vegetable shortening
2 cups sugar
3 eggs
2 cups all-purpose flour
½ teaspoon salt
½ cup buttermilk or sour milk
Chopped nuts, if desired

FUDGE FROSTING
2 cups granulated sugar
1 cup packed brown sugar
3 tablespoons unsweetened cocoa powder
About 1 ½ cups light cream
3 tablespoons light corn syrup

Who wouldn't take the devil's dare when it comes to eating this fudge-topped treat? I've never found another cake as all-around good as this one. I've had the recipe since I was in third grade, when a one-room schoolhouse near my father's farm held a fundraiser. Among the events was a cakewalk—and I won three cakes that night! My mother let me keep just one, and this was the one I chose. It was so wonderful that I asked the baker, Phoebe Schwartz, to share the recipe with me.

Preheat oven to 350°F. Grease and flour-dust 2 round 9-inch baking pans or a 9 x 13-inch baking pan. In a bowl, mix cocoa and boiling water until smoothly blended. Stir in baking soda and vanilla, and set aside.

In large bowl of an electric mixer, cream shortening and sugar on medium speed. Increase mixer speed to medium-high. Add eggs, 1 at a time, beating until smooth after each addition. In another bowl, combine flour and salt. Add to creamed mixture alternately with buttermilk or sour milk, beating with mixer on low speed after each addition. Then beat on medium speed until smooth and well blended. Add cocoa mixture and beat until blended. Pour into prepared pans. Bake 35 to 45 minutes or until a wooden pick inserted in center of cake comes out clean. Cool layers in pans for 5 minutes, and then turn out onto cooling rack to cool completely. (Cool sheet cake in pan.)

To prepare Fudge Frosting, mix sugars and cocoa in a saucepan. Stir in cream and corn syrup. Bring to a boil over medium heat, stirring. Boil without stirring until mixture reaches soft-ball stage, about 135°F, and then remove from heat. Beat vigorously, adding more cream as needed to make a creamy, spreadable frosting. Frost cake while icing is still warm. Sprinkle frosted cake with chopped nuts, if desired.

Makes 1 (9-inch) layer cake or 1 (9 x 13-inch) sheet cake

Ginger Fudge Pudding

Chocolate lovers will dream about this yummy pudding-like cake—especially if they like the excitement of ginger, which is amazingly healthful.

Preheat the oven to 375°F, checking to make sure the rack is in the center position. In a microwave, melt butter and chocolate together for about 1 minute, or until they are just melted. Or, place in a saucepan and cook, stirring, over low heat until melted, about 3 to 5 minutes. Cool until mixture is no longer hot and is just warm to the touch. Set aside.

Using a mixer or whisk, beat the eggs and sugar until the sugar is completely dissolved and mixture is light and lemon colored. Add cooled chocolate-butter mixture and combine until well mixed.

Sift together the cocoa powder and cornstarch. Grind ginger in food processor with a small amount of the dry ingredients until small pieces form. Combine the remaining dry ingredients together. Add dry ingredients, about ¼ at a time to the butter mixture, beating well after each addition.

Butter a 9-inch round spring form pan, line the bottom with a buttered waxed paper circle, and flour the pan. Pour batter into pan and bake in a warm water bath, which is done by placing the cake pan in a larger pan, and adding warm water to about the 1-inch level. Bake for 40 to 45 minutes, or until just firm.

Meanwhile, prepare the Whipped Cream Topping. Place the cream in the mixer bowl and add sugar. Beat on highest speed until stiff. Set aside until cake is ready.

Cool the cake at room temperature, and then invert the pan and remove cake. Chill cake in the refrigerator until cool to the touch. Add whipped cream topping. Sprinkle with candied ginger, dust with cocoa powder, and serve.

⇥ Makes 1 (9-inch) cake

1 cup butter
8 ounces unsweetened chocolate
5 eggs
1 ⅓ cups sugar
⅛ cup cocoa powder
¼ cup cornstarch
⅓ cup crystallized ginger
2 tablespoons candied ginger, chopped
1 tablespoon cocoa powder

WHIPPED CREAM TOPPING
½ cup whipping cream
2 tablespoons sugar

Jam Cake

4 cups all-purpose flour

2 teaspoons baking soda

½ cup unsalted butter, room temperature

2 cups sugar

6 eggs, separated

2 teaspoons ground cloves

2 teaspoons ground nutmeg

2 teaspoons ground allspice

2 teaspoons ground cinnamon

2 cups seedless blackberry jam

1 cup sour milk or buttermilk

FILLING

½ cup unsalted butter

2 cups sugar

2 cups milk

Norma Jean Ross shared this traditional Tennessee recipe with me, saying her family almost always prepares it at holiday time. It's a rich, spicy cake that's excellent with coffee, milk, or eggnog.

Preheat oven to 375°F. Grease 3 round 9-inch or 4 round 8-inch baking pans; line pans with waxed paper. Lightly grease paper.

Sift together flour and baking soda. Set aside. In a large bowl of an electric mixer, cream butter and sugar on medium speed. In a small bowl, beat egg yolks well. Blend into creamed mixture along with cloves, nutmeg, allspice, cinnamon, and jam. Add flour mixture alternately with sour milk or buttermilk, beating until smooth after each addition.

In a small bowl, beat egg whites until they hold stiff peaks. Carefully fold into batter. Pour batter into prepared pans. Bake 35 to 40 minutes, or until a wooden pick inserted in center of cake comes out clean. Cool in pans 5 minutes, and then turn cake out of pans onto cooling racks. Peel off paper and cool completely.

To prepare Filling, combine all filling ingredients in a medium saucepan. Cook over medium heat, stirring, 15 to 20 minutes, or until mixture begins to thicken. To assemble cake, stack layers, spreading hot filling between layers and on top of cake. ⚕ Makes 1 (8- or 9-inch) layer cake

Poppy Seed Torte

A Hungarian lady living in Albuquerque gave me this recipe. A terrific cook, she inherited the recipe from her mother, who always made poppy seed cake for special occasions. The contrasting textures of crunchy poppy seeds and smooth, soothing custard make the dessert a real delight.

Soak poppy seeds in milk several hours or overnight. Preheat oven to 375°F. Butter 3 round 8-inch baking pans, and then line with waxed paper. Lightly butter paper.

Sift together flour, baking powder, and salt. Set aside. In a large bowl of an electric mixer, cream ½ cup butter and sugar on medium speed. Add poppy seed-milk mixture to creamed mixture alternately with flour mixture, beating until well blended after each addition. In a small bowl, beat egg whites until they hold soft peaks. Fold into batter. Spread batter in prepared pans. Bake 25 to 30 minutes, and then turn cake out of pans onto cooling racks. Peel off paper and cool completely.

Meanwhile, prepare Custard Filling. In a saucepan, stir together sugar, salt, and cornstarch. Gradually stir in milk, and then egg yolks. Cook over medium heat, stirring constantly, until thickened. Cool slightly, and stir in vanilla and black walnuts. To assemble cake, stack layers, spreading filling between layers and on top of cake.

⇥ Makes 1 (8-inch) layer cake

¾ cup poppy seeds

1 ¼ cups milk

About 1 tablespoon unsalted butter, room temperature

2 ¾ cups all-purpose flour

1 ½ teaspoons baking powder

¼ teaspoon salt

½ cup unsalted butter, room temperature

1 ¼ cups sugar

4 egg whites

CUSTARD FILLING

½ cup sugar

¼ teaspoon salt

1 tablespoon cornstarch

1 ½ cups milk

4 egg yolks, well beaten

¾ teaspoon Mexican vanilla extract or 1 teaspoon regular vanilla extract

½ cup coarsely chopped black walnuts

Steve's Skillet Cake

½ cup unsalted butter
1 cup milk
1 cup sugar
1 cup all-purpose flour
Freshly grated nutmeg, to taste
½ teaspoon salt
½ teaspoon baking powder
2 cups fresh fruit, such as berries, sliced
  peaches, or sliced apricots
½ cup dairy sour cream, if desired

This cake is so easy you won't believe it! It is a 5-minute wonder and truly delicious for dessert or brunch. Steve Bryant, a restaurateur, often makes it with huckleberries from his yard—but other fruits are equally good.

Preheat oven to 375°F. Set butter in a heavy 9-inch skillet with an ovenproof handle. Place skillet in oven until butter is melted.

Meanwhile, in a bowl, beat together milk, sugar, flour, nutmeg, salt, and baking powder with a whisk until smooth and free of lumps. Stir melted butter into batter, and then pour batter back into skillet. Place fruit in center of batter and bake about 30 minutes, or until top of cake is browned and fruit is tender. Serve warm, with sour cream, if desired.
⊰ Makes 6 to 8 servings

Orange Blossom Blueberry Pie

Rich pastry for a double-crust 9-inch pie
5 cups fresh blueberries
1 ½ cups sugar
⅓ cup all-purpose flour
1 navel orange, unpeeled and thinly sliced
¼ cup Grand Marnier
½ teaspoon ground cinnamon
Freshly grated nutmeg, to taste
2 tablespoons unsalted butter
2 tablespoons milk

Fragrant and tangy with fresh orange and orange liqueur, this spicy pie is one of our family favorites. We like it served plain, but you might also try it with a scoop of rich vanilla ice cream melting over each slice.

Set oven rack in lowest position. Preheat oven to 425°F. Roll out half the pastry and use to line a 9-inch pie plate. Fill pastry shell with blueberries. Combine all but 1 tablespoon of the sugar with flour and sprinkle evenly over berries. Cut each orange slice in half, and then arrange half-slices uniformly around edge of pie. Pour Grand Marnier evenly over top. Sprinkle with cinnamon and nutmeg. Dot with butter. Roll out remaining pastry, and place on pie. Seal and flute edges, and cut steam vents. Brush top crust with milk, and then sprinkle with reserved 1 tablespoon sugar and a few grates of nutmeg. Bake 15 minutes, reduce oven temperature to 375°F, and continue to bake 30 minutes longer, or until crust is lightly browned and filling is bubbly. Serve warm. ⊰ Makes 1 (9-inch) pie

Pink Adobe French Apple Pie

This is, by far, the very best apple pie I've ever tasted—rich, spicy, embellished with raisins and pecans, and topped with creamy Rum or Brandy Hard Sauce. Rosalea, owner and founder of the famous Pink Adobe Restaurant in Santa Fe, created this recipe ages ago; it has proved so popular she can hardly keep up with the demand. Regular patrons frequently order it when they first arrive at the restaurant or even when they make their reservations, just to be sure they'll have a piece! Once you sample this recipe, you'll be preparing it often. The pie freezes beautifully, so always make at least two at a time.

Set oven rack in lowest position. Preheat oven to 450°F. Roll out half the pastry and use to line a 9-inch pie plate. Place apples in pastry shell, mounding them toward center. Sprinkle with lemon juice, nutmeg, and cinnamon. Spread 6 tablespoons of the granulated sugar and raisins evenly over apples.

In a separate bowl, mix brown sugar, flour, and butter until well blended, and then spread over apples. Sprinkle with pecans, and add 3 tablespoons of the milk. Roll out remaining pastry and place on pie. Seal and flute edges, and cut steam vents. Brush top curst with remaining milk, and sprinkle with remaining granulated sugar. Bake 10 minutes, and then reduce oven temperature to 350°F. Continue to bake 30 minutes longer, or until crust is golden brown and filling is bubbly.

Meanwhile, prepare the Rum or Brandy Hard Sauce. In a medium bowl, cream butter until fluffy, add powdered sugar and boiling water, and beat until well blended. Beat in rum or brandy. Set aside.

Cool pie briefly, and then cut in wedges. Serve on warmed plates topped with hard sauce. Let each slice stand a few minutes before serving, so sauce has time to melt down into filling. ⚞ Makes 1 (9-inch) pie

Pastry for a double-crust 9-inch pie
1 pound cooking apples, peeled, cored, and sliced
2 tablespoons lemon juice
½ teaspoon ground nutmeg
½ teaspoon ground cinnamon
½ cup granulated sugar
¼ cup raisins
1 cup packed light brown sugar
2 tablespoons all-purpose flour
2 tablespoons unsalted butter, cut in small pieces
½ cup pecan halves
¼ cup milk

RUM OR BRANDY HARD SAUCE
½ cup unsalted butter, room temperature
1 ½ cups powdered sugar
1 tablespoon boiling water
1 teaspoon rum or brandy

Christmas Cardinale Bombe

1 quart vanilla ice cream
1 ½ pints pistachio ice cream
1 pint raspberry sherbet
½ cup shelled unsalted pistachio nuts,
    coarsely chopped (see Note)
Fresh raspberries, if desired
Fresh mint sprigs, if desired

RASPBERRY SAUCE
2 (12- to 14-ounce) packages frozen
    unsweetened raspberries, thawed and
    undrained
¼ cup sugar
⅓ cup Framboise or kirsch

*Note: If you can't find unsalted pistachios, simmer
salted pistachios briefly in plenty of water, rinse
thoroughly, and dry well.*

So gorgeous to look at and yet so easy to make—this beautiful dessert seems almost too good to believe! It's perfect for parties, especially those with a Mexican theme, since it sports Mexico's national colors of red, white, and green. The Raspberry Sauce that tops each slice is good on plain ice cream, cakes, and pies, too.

A day or so before serving, put a 3-quart bombe mold or metal bowl in freezer for at least 30 minutes. Remove vanilla ice cream from freezer, and set in refrigerator until soft but not melted. Using a spatula and working rapidly, line frozen mold or bowl evenly with vanilla ice cream. Immediately return mold or bowl to freezer, and freeze until vanilla ice cream is firm.

Meanwhile, place pistachio ice cream in refrigerator until soft but not melted. Smooth a uniform layer of pistachio ice cream over firm layer of vanilla, and then immediately return to freezer until firm.

Place sherbet in refrigerator until soft but not melted. Fill center of mold with sherbet, and quickly return to freezer at least 3 hours. Also, freeze a serving plate or platter until very cold.

To unmold, dip mold or bowl in hot water to rim. Invert on frozen plate or platter. Lift off mold. Carefully stud bombe with pistachios, being sure to cover outside surface uniformly. Immediately return to freezer until ready to serve.

To prepare Raspberry Sauce, combine all sauce ingredients in a saucepan. Bring to a simmer, and simmer over low heat for 3 minutes. Pour into a food processor and process until smooth. Push through a fine sieve.

To serve, heat a knife in hot water, dry off, and then cut a slice of bombe. Continue to slice, heating and drying knife before each cut. Drizzle each serving with Raspberry Sauce and garnish with fresh raspberries and mint, if desired.
⤚Makes 10 to 12 servings

Peach Kabobs

When peaches are in their prime, try this simple dessert. It is quick, easy, delicious, and great on the grill, making a perfect ending for a grilled meal. Have fun serving them crisscrossed over rich French vanilla ice cream, peach ice cream, or mango or raspberry sorbet. For a striking dessert for a small group, make the kabobs small and stab them into the ice cream or sorbet in a footed dessert glass.

Rinse, halve, and slice open the peaches, removing the pits. Combine the orange juice, lime juice, honey, and nutmeg in a small bowl. Taste and determine if more honey is needed. Pour over sliced peaches and mix well to coat. Thread skewers through peaches and grill until peaches are warm and edges are a bit browned. ⚞ Makes 4 servings

4 ripe freestone peaches, slightly firm to the touch
½ orange, juiced
1 lime, juiced
1 tablespoon honey, or to taste
Fresh nutmeg, to taste

Dessert Fondue

6 ounces unsweetened chocolate

1 cup light cream

1 ¼ cups sugar

½ cup unsalted butter

2 teaspoons Mexican vanilla extract or 1 tablespoon regular vanilla extract

Fruits and/or cakes of your choice, such as strawberries, fresh or canned pineapple wedges, banana slices, apple wedges, orange segments, pound or butter cake cubes, angel food or sponge cake cubes, or slices of ladyfingers

A delightful ending for any meal, this sweet fondue also makes a convivial mid-afternoon or late-evening snack. Just dip your choice of fruit and fresh baked goods in this rich, easy-to-make sauce. The only secret is to watch the cooking temperature closely; any heat above medium-low will cause the chocolate to bind (clump up).

Place chocolate, cream, sugar, and butter in a heavy saucepan or fondue pot. Stir constantly over medium-low heat until smoothly melted. Continue to cook, stirring, about 5 minutes, or until thickened. Stir in vanilla. To serve, attractively arrange mounds of fruits and cakes on a tray. Let guests spear fruits and cake cubes with long fondue forks or dinner forks, and then dunk each morsel in chocolate.

⌇ Makes 6 to 8 servings

Hawaiian Double Coconut Parfaits

½ pound crushed butter pecan cookies or vanilla wafers

½ cup melted butter

½ cup shredded or flaked coconut

1 cup milk

1 cup Coco Lopez or similar coconut cream

⅓ cup all-purpose flour

About ⅔ cup sugar

2 large eggs, slightly beaten

1 ½ cups shredded or flaked coconut

1 teaspoon Mexican vanilla

¼ cup shredded or flaked coconut, toasted (see Note)

WHIPPED TOPPING

1 cup whipping cream

⅓ cup granulated sugar

½ teaspoon Mexican vanilla

Note: To toast coconut, place on a baking sheet and bake at 350°F until slightly brown.

Following a spicy meal, nothing could be better than a creamy coconut pie served in a tall, slender wine glass or sour glass, especially if you like coconut. If you have fresh coconuts available and the time, try substituting fresh grated coconut for the shredded coconut in this recipe. If you would rather have a pie than a parfait, just press the flavored crumbs into a 9-inch pie plate.

In a large bowl, combine the crushed cookies or wafers, melted butter, and ½ cup coconut. Set crumbs aside.

In a heavy 3-quart saucepan, warm milk and cream together over medium heat. In a small bowl, mix together flour and sugar. When the milk is warm, gradually stir in flour mixture, whisking constantly. Cook until thick. Cool, and add the eggs. Add the 1 ½ cups coconut and vanilla. Combine well and set pudding aside. If desired, prepare Whipped Topping. Place cream in a mixer bowl and add sugar and vanilla. Beat on highest speed until stiff.

Using slender, tall parfait or wine glasses, layer crumbs and pudding, in that order, ending with pudding. If desired, top with Whipped Topping, making pretty swirls. Scatter with toasted coconut and serve immediately.

⌇ Makes 6 to 8 servings

2 tablespoons sugar

About 1 tablespoon lime zest

½ fresh lime, cut into wedges

1 (14-ounce) can sweetened condensed
  milk

2 tablespoons orange liqueur, such as
  Triple Sec

3 tablespoons tequila

⅓ cup fresh lime juice

1 cup whipping cream

Donna's Margarita Mousse

This delicious, fluffy dessert melts in your mouth and is a
snap to make. And the presentation of this mousse served
in sugar-rimmed margarita glasses is delightful!

In a small bowl, combine sugar with 1 teaspoon of the lime
zest. Gently rub the rims of 4 to 6 margarita glasses with
lime wedges to moisten, crunch into granulated sugar mixture, and place in the freezer.

In a separate bowl, combine remaining lime zest, condensed milk, Triple Sec, tequila, and ⅓ cup lime juice. Set
aside. Whip cream until stiff peaks form. Fold whipped cream
into tequila mixture, working carefully to keep the air in the
whipped cream. Spoon into prepared frozen glasses, making
sure not to disturb the sugared rims. Refrigerate for 4 hours,
or until firm. ⤙ Makes 4 to 6 servings

Butterscotch Peach Crisp

About 1 tablespoon unsalted butter, room temperature

1 cup packed brown sugar

1 cup all-purpose flour

¼ teaspoon ground cinnamon

⅛ teaspoon ground nutmeg

¼ cup finely diced crystallized ginger

½ cup solid vegetable shortening or unsalted butter

2 cups fresh or frozen unsweetened sliced peaches or other fruit (thaw frozen fruit just until mushy, and then pull apart with a fork)

Crunchy, gooey, and wonderful! The spicy crystallized ginger really adds to the flavor. You can substitute other fruits for the peaches—try apricots, any kind of berry, plums, or rhubarb. If you don't mind the calories, top the crisp with whipped cream or ice cream.

Preheat oven to 375°F. Butter an 8-inch square baking dish. In a medium bowl, combine brown sugar, flour, cinnamon, nutmeg, and ginger. Cut in shortening or butter until mixture resembles coarse crumbs. Spread fruit in buttered baking dish, and then sprinkle with crumb mixture. Bake, uncovered, for 35 to 40 minutes, or until fruit is soft and crumb topping is brown. ⚞ Makes 4 to 6 servings

Belgian Dessert Waffles

1 cup sifted all-purpose flour

2 teaspoons sugar

1 teaspoon baking powder

¼ teaspoon baking soda

¼ teaspoon salt

1 egg, separated

1 cup dairy sour cream

½ cup milk

3 tablespoons unsalted butter, melted

STRAWBERRY SAUCE

1 cup hulled fresh strawberries or frozen sweetened strawberries (thaw frozen berries slightly, and then pull apart with a fork)

1 tablespoon sugar (omit if using frozen berries)

2 tablespoons brandy, if desired

ICE CREAM FLUFF

1 cup whipping cream

1 cup vanilla ice cream

These delicious waffles make a super ending to a spicy meal. Serve them with two toppings: Ice Cream Fluff, a luscious blend of whipped cream and vanilla ice cream, and rosy Strawberry Sauce.

To prepare Strawberry Sauce, combine all sauce ingredients in a blender. Process on low speed a few seconds or just until berries are coarsely chopped. Let stand about 1 hour at room temperature or heat over low heat about 15 minutes. Set aside.

Preheat a waffle baker to medium-high. Sift together flour, sugar, baking powder, baking soda, and salt. Set aside.

In a small bowl of an electric mixer, beat egg white until it holds very stiff peaks. In a large bowl of a mixer, beat egg yolk, sour cream, milk, and melted butter until blended. Blend flour mixture into egg yolk mixture, beating with mixer on low speed. Increase mixer speed to medium-high and beat until smooth. Fold in beaten egg white. Bake batter in pre-heated waffle baker until waffles are golden brown and crisp.

Meanwhile, prepare Ice Cream Fluff. In a large bowl of an electric mixer, beat whipping cream on high speed until thickened but not stiff enough to hold its shape. Add ice cream, a spoonful at a time, beating just until smooth after each addition. To serve, top each hot waffle with Ice Cream Fluff and Strawberry Sauce. ⚞ Makes 2 (10-inch) waffles

Sumptuous Chocolate-Walnut Soufflé

Hot from the oven, this luscious, fudgy soufflé is first sparked with flaming cognac, and then topped with spoonfuls of whipped cream laced with cognac. For truly outrageous indulgence, drizzle Red Raspberry Revel Sauce prettily over the cream. (For the best flavor, be sure to use a good-quality cognac such as Courvoisier in the soufflé, cream, and sauce.)

Generously butter a 10-inch Bundt pan using the 1 to 2 tablespoons butter. In a bowl, combine walnuts, milk, and vanilla. Set aside.

Place egg yolks in a blender, food processor, or large bowl. Add salt and sugar, and process or whisk until well blended. Add the 2 ½ tablespoons melted butter and process or whisk again until blended. If using a blender or food processor, add milk-nut mixture to yolk mixture and process until well puréed. If using a whisk, grind milk-nut mixture in a food mill, and then whisk into yolk mixture. Set aside.

In a heavy saucepan over very low heat or in a double boiler over simmering water, carefully melt chocolate, stirring constantly. Remove from heat. Preheat oven to 350°F. Beat egg whites with cream of tartar until the mixture holds very stiff peaks. Fold melted chocolate into yolk-nut mixture, and then fold in egg whites, being careful to maintain volume. Gently fold in 3 tablespoons cognac, rum, and whisky. Turn mixture into buttered pan. Bake 30 minutes, or until a knife inserted in center comes out clean.

Meanwhile, prepare Cognac-Laced Whipped Cream. In a chilled bowl, beat cream until foamy. Gradually add sugar in a thin stream, beating constantly. Add cognac and continue to beat until cream is very stiff. Cover and refrigerate.

To make Red Raspberry Revel Sauce, combine raspberries, sugar, and butter in a small, heavy saucepan. Cook, stirring, about 5 minutes, or until raspberries are hot and juice is sweet. Turn off heat and stir in cognac. Hold at room temperature until serving.

When soufflé is done, cool a few minutes, and then carefully turn out onto a platter. Heat ¼ cup cognac in a small saucepan, carefully flame, and drizzle over soufflé. Serve soufflé very hot topped with Cognac-Laced Whipping Cream and Red Raspberry Revel Sauce. ⌐ Makes 8 servings

1 to 2 tablespoons unsalted butter, room temperature

1 ½ cups coarsely broken English walnuts (not black walnuts)

¾ cup whole milk

1 teaspoon Mexican vanilla extract or 1½ teaspoons regular vanilla extract

4 egg yolks

Dash of salt

6 tablespoons sugar

2 ½ tablespoons unsalted butter, melted

6 ounces unsweetened chocolate

5 egg whites

¼ teaspoon cream of tartar

3 tablespoons cognac

1 teaspoon rum

1 teaspoon whisky

¼ cup cognac

COGNAC-LACED WHIPPED CREAM

1 cup whipping cream

¼ cup sugar

1 tablespoon cognac

RED RASPBERRY REVEL SAUCE

2 cups fresh raspberries or frozen unsweetened raspberries, thawed and undrained

¼ cup sugar

2 tablespoons unsalted butter

1 tablespoon cognac

Index

Note: Italic page numbers indicate photographs

HAVE FUN LEARNING THE
HOTTEST
TASTE IN AMERICA

Purest chiles, herbs and ingredients
from our Pecos Valley Spice Co.
To Order, pecosvalley.com

Join our Cooking Club, www.janebutel.com
Watch our television show,
Jane Butel's Southwestern Kitchen on PBS

Mention this advertisement when you call for a special discount or gift.

Learn With The Best!
Jane Butel and her professional cooking school staff.

Jane Butel, Internationally renowned teacher, first to write about
Southwestern cooking, best-selling author, television personality
and America's foremost authority on Southwestern cooking.

In beautiful Albuquerque, New Mexico 1-800-472-8229 www.janebutel.com

JANE BUTEL, a native of New Mexico, is an internationally recognized authority on the regional cooking of the American Southwest. She was the first to write about the cooking style that evolved in the southwestern border area, and is credited with starting our nation's love affair with this cuisine. Since the release of her first cookbook in 1961, she has continued to explore the region's unique ingredients, recipes, and cooking techniques. In all, she has written 16 cookbooks, including 6 best-sellers.

In 1983, she founded the Jane Butel's Southwestern School in Santa Fe, moving to Albuquerque in 1993, which was recognized by *Bon Appétit* magazine as one of the best vacation cooking schools in the world. Ms. Butel is also the founder of Pecos Valley Spice Co., a trusted source for chiles, spices, and other authentic southwestern ingredients, and Jane Butel Corporation. Through her writing, teaching, and television projects, she continues to season this country's melting pot with the rich culinary, cultural, and historical heritage of the Southwest.

To register or for information about Jane Butel's Cooking School, call 800-472-8229 or e-mail www.janebutel.com.

MAIL ORDER SOURCES

Pecos Valley Spice Co.
Albuquerque, NM 87102
800-473-Taco (8226)
www.pecosvalley.com

Pendery's
Dallas, TX 75027
800-533-1870
www.penderys.com